'Jo Saxton is one of the best communicators of the
Christian faith I know. She is faithful to the Scriptures,
she's relevant to today's world, and she links the two
superbly. REAL GOD, REAL LIFE, like its author,
does just this.'

Mike Pilavachi

Also by Jo Saxton:

Influential: Women in Leadership at Church, Work and Beyond

Real God, Real Life

Finding a spirituality that works

JO SAXTON

HODDER

First published in Great Britain in 2010 by Hodder & Stoughton
An Hachette UK company

This paperback edition published in 2011

1

A CIP catalogue record for this title is available from the British Library

ISBN 978 0 340 99529 7

Typeset in Adobe Garamond by Ellipsis Digital Limited, Glasgow

Printed and bound by Clays Ltd, St Ives plc

Hodder & Stoughton policy is to use papers that are natural,
renewable and recyclable products and made from wood grown in
sustainable forests. The logging and manufacturing processes are expected
to conform to the environmental regulations of the country of origin.

Hodder & Stoughton Ltd
338 Euston Road
London NW1 3BH

www.hodderfaith.com

AN APPRECIATION

Margaret and Maurice Morton,
Andrew Lund, Alf Waite,
Ros Lund, Carole Pattenden,
Mike and Sally Breen.
For more than you'll ever know.

Contents

Thank you!   1

Foreword   3

Introduction: Scandal or transformation?   5

1. Follow me   11

2. In training   27

SECTION ONE: HEART PRACTICES

3. Practising surrender   39

4. Practising forgiveness   51

5. How to practise in pain   65

6. Practising thanksgiving   83

SECTION TWO: PRACTISING LIFE

7. Deserts and shipwrecks   105

8. Connecting with God   129

9. **The life together – a glimpse of His glory**   149

10. **Sometimes you can't make it on your own**   165

11. **A walk across the park**   183

12. **Lifesaver**   201

Epilogue: Keep running   219

Notes   223

Thank you!

So many people to thank; so little space. I hope I remember everyone, and I hope this is not too reminiscent of a lengthy awards acceptance speech!

This book began as a seminar series at Soul Survivor and Momentum, where we sought to work out how to live for God with all that we are and have in everyday life. So my love and thanks to the Soul Survivor gang and to the delegates who helped ignite something in me . . .

Thanks to 'Team Hodder' – especially Wendy, Claire and the legendary Katherine Venn ('KV') for your support and friendship and for taking an idea and making me run with it. You've been so encouraging, positive and committed and you've even laughed at my jokes. And thanks to my friends who've helped me keep going, especially Susan Miller – you're one of a kind! To my friends who looked after my drafts, read them and gave feedback, Zan, Bry, Tracy: Mwah!

I'm a talker, so even though I'm writing alone, I've needed people to process ideas with. Special thanks to Mal Calladine, Steve Cockram, Toby Bassford and Dr Grayson Carter, Ben and Helen Askew, Martin Garner and Jen Eckersall (I know that's a lot of people – I told you I'm a talker!) for listening and sharing your wisdom as work got underway.

I'm grateful to all the wonderful people who've shared practical ideas in this book. You're fab! And I'd like to give a special mention to those who shared their personal stories about their walk with God. Thanks for your vulnerability and your honesty.

Finally, my biggest love and thanks are for my family. To my amazing husband Chris, for your constant support and encouragement, and to Tia and Zoë our fantastic daughters – I love you THIS much!

Foreword

Some years back I was looking for a personal trainer. I had always been familiar with the disciplines of physical fitness but felt that my interest was waning, and with a busy life I needed someone to take me to a stage that I could not reach on my own. I asked for recommendations. The person I chose not only had the same name as me, but was like me in many ways – he seemed to know instantly what I needed and how to get me there. In the midst of a stressful life, whilst under his tutelage, I maintained a level of health and fitness I had not reached before.

When it comes to our spiritual lives, most of us will need a personal trainer too. Joannah Saxton is that person.

A good trainer tells you the bad news as well as the good. There is lots of encouragement here, but also much reality. If we are determined to follow Jesus in every part of our lives, we must face the consequences of a life that is not fully engaged with Him.

Joannah knows what you are thinking and what you need. She understands the best practices to grow and maintain your spiritual health. She is an expert in the spiritual life and as you follow her simple principles and turn them into a practical regimen for your own life, you will receive untold benefits.

You will not find here the trite simplicity of a checklist but rather the profound simplicity of ageless wisdom applied to real life. Alongside this, there is a constant call to balance, connecting our relationship with God to those with whom we share our lives, and to those for whom we need to invest our lives. With our life in balance, we attain a sense of inner poise that leads to a tangible experience of personal peace.

I have watched the effect of this in the lives of people blessed to have been mentored by Joannah – including my own children. Within the pages of this book, you will find tried and tested truths of the spiritual life seen in the lives of the great saints down through the ages emanating from the life of Jesus Himself. This book will prove to be a great adventure, a worthwhile journey and as you look back, a great gift from the hands of the Lord Himself.

Mike Breen
Senior Guardian, The Order of Mission
South Carolina

Introduction:
Scandal or transformation

I came so they can have real and eternal life, more and better life than they ever dreamed of.
(John 10:10 *The Message*)

Q. Does Jesus transform a person's life?

SCANDALOUS

I was browsing through my local library when one book in particular grabbed my attention. I simply couldn't resist it. The title alone, *The Scandal of the Evangelical Conscience*,[1] had me hooked.

The introduction explored research concerning the lives of Christians in the Western world, focusing on America in particular. They were people who called themselves 'evangelical', 'born again', or who expressed some degree of commitment to Christ. Yet the research discovered that issues such as divorce, domestic violence, abortion, adultery and pornography were often as common among Christians as among non-Christians. They looked at the capacity Christians alone had in their giving to change the face of global debt, even if they just tithed – yet found that they gave a small amount. The statistics just kept on coming.

Divorce is more common among 'born again' Christians than in the general American population. Only 6 percent of evangelicals tithe. White evangelicals are *the* most likely to object to neighbors of another race.[2]

These were in the opening chapters, and I didn't have the stomach to read on. I was embarrassed and humbled. How has knowing Jesus Christ made so little difference to our daily lives? I wanted to get on my knees and cry loudly and tell God how sorry I was. But of course I didn't; libraries are supposed to be quiet places. I was concerned that people might think I was a crazy woman, crying out to God like that. So I walked away sad and fundamentally unsettled. And wondering why I couldn't get down on my knees and cry out to God in the library of a theological college. I don't blame the college for that. The inhibition was all mine, and it was scandalous.

GREAT GIFTS MEAN GREAT RESPONSIBILITIES

In Luke 12, Jesus tells the story of the master who entrusts his servant with his household. Jesus outlines two ways in which the servant responds to the task. If the servant is a 'faithful and wise manager',[3] he attends to his responsibilities and receives more as a result. The second response, however, is something else! Knowing his master won't return for a long time, the servant becomes passive, lazy and then greedy. He abuses his fellow servants and goes out eating and drinking. His actions catch up with him when his master returns unexpectedly, and the servant pays a high price. Jesus concludes the story with the words:

> From everyone who has been given much, much will be
> demanded; and from the one who has been entrusted with
> much, much more will be asked.[4]

This parable found in Luke offers the Western Church a sobering challenge. *The Message* translation of this passage reads, 'Great gifts mean great responsibilities; greater gifts, greater responsibilities!'[5] The Church in the Western world has been given so much! We have incredible resources. We have church buildings and TV stations, music and books, conferences and festivals. Even in times of financial difficulty, we have much more than churches in many other parts of the world. We have also been blessed with freedom to be Christians, something that comes so naturally to us it's easy to take it for granted. So what have we done with the gifts we've been given? Have we been wise and faithful?

Or have we become passive in our faith, lazy, even greedy, keeping the good news and all the riches of heaven we enjoy to ourselves while letting others starve? What have we done with the incredible resources we've been given? What have we done with the message that has been entrusted to us?

Is it making a difference? Are we making a difference?

If we spent an hour watching the national or international news, we'd be inundated with opportunities to make a difference. With God's resources and guidance, what could we do about our inner cities, human trafficking, poverty, AIDS? What could we do about the huge numbers of people who have never heard of God's love? Europe birthed a Reformation and other huge Christian movements in the past, yet today in many cities (in the UK at least) churches have become beautiful stained-glass history, converted into lecture theatres, pubs and studio apartments. So is a faith that is real and effective now history too?

FACING THE POINTING FINGER

Yet for all that Ronald Sider, author of *The Scandal of the Evangelical Conscience*, wrote about the Western Church at large, the biggest challenge I found in that library that afternoon was personal. It reminded me that our churches are made up of lots of people like me. When the question of the Western Church's effectiveness is asked, or when I consider Jesus' words from Luke's Gospel, pointing a finger elsewhere is a weak response. It is easy to judge statistics representing people I've never met, whose lives I've never known. But there is one life I know only too well, and that's where I need to take a closer look. I need to start with me. Is my faith real and vital today, or is it history?

I have to admit that sometimes, like the people those statistics represent, there is a chasm between what I say that I believe and what I live that I believe. There are days when I'm still a slave to habits and attitudes that I have sung (in both chorus and hymn form) about being abundantly free from. I will sing them again, because I do want to be free! I want to be free from the days when unforgiveness and bitterness shape my attitudes and my actions. I want to be free from the times when my pride swings violently between delusions of superiority and delusions of abject inferiority.

Sometimes I'm controlled by ordinary everyday things. It might be a need for approval that results in people-pleasing tendencies in my relationships; or a negative thought pattern that spirals and ignites a short-fused temper. It could be working too hard for too long because I have something to prove, and my family pay the price, again. I know they are ordinary, everyday things, yet sometimes they seem to have such a vice-like grip. In times like these I wonder if this is as good as it gets as a Christian: you hope to live and be better, but have a sneaking feeling that in reality it's just more of the same old you. I'd much rather have the real and eternal life that Jesus promises!

REAL GOD FOR REAL LIFE

Thankfully, it's not all dependent on us. It never was. God is real, and in His Son Jesus Christ He reached down and rescued us, though we may not even have realised we were drowning. He initiated a relationship with us that does have the potential to transform our existence. So when we think of resources that shape our faith, the greatest 'resource' we will ever have is a relationship with a living God. It's a relationship for every situation in life. God is real for the good parts of our lives that we love and enjoy; good times with friends and family, a promotion at work. He's real in the mundane parts of life; when we simply endure the repetition of a job we don't particularly enjoy but need, or when we're bored by the drudgery of our daily tasks and responsibilities. God is real in the desperate parts of our lives; when our marriages and friendships struggle, or when we feel mounting financial pressure with no way out. God is real when unfulfilled dreams end in disappointment; in terrible dark days of tragedy and loss. Our lives may not be picture perfect or straightforward, yet our God is interested in every detail, wanting to meet us there. Our responsibility lies in how we respond to the relationship He offers us.

> I came so they can have real and eternal life, more and better life than they ever dreamed of.[6]

Jesus promised us *life*. It's a life that doesn't just begin when we die, but starts now. We have a real God for real life.

1

Follow me

*Are you tired? Worn out? Burned out on religion? Come to
me. Get away with me and you'll recover your life. I'll show
you how to take a real rest. Walk with me and work with me
– watch how I do it. Learn the unforced rhythms of grace.*
(Matthew 11:28–9 *The Message*)

Follow me.
(Matthew 9:9)

**Q. So how do we do this life with God? How do we grow and
mature spiritually?**

DIVERSE CHURCH, DIVERSE CHRISTIANS

Christians throughout history have responded to the challenges
of their culture by exploring afresh how to cultivate their faith for
a new day. In doing so they developed practices that would transform their fellow believers and change the world in which they
lived. Today in the twenty-first century we can look back at two
thousand years of a rich global Christian heritage, stories of
Christians who embraced God in everyday life. They were African
men and women in the desert, Celtic men and women living in
communities, Italian monks and English mystics. They were
reformers, church leaders, lawyers, theologians, politicians turned
priests, abolitionists. Some were well known; many were anony-
mous. Some walked away from their wealth and others invested

their wealth for the kingdom's cause. They were people who dreamed dreams and had visions. They were among the civil rights activists in the USA in the 1960s and the anti-apartheid activists in South Africa in the 1980s. They birthed movements, reminding the wider body of Christ of facets of the gospel they may have forgotten, such as a missionary zeal with a global perspective or a passion for the poorest in society. They were history-makers. The history of the Church illustrates how it is possible to love a real God with a real life. Yet it also illustrates incredible diversity in how Christians developed their relationship with God.

The same rich diversity is evident across the Church globally today. Our Church traditions emphasise a number of ways in which we can nurture our life with God. While some stress the value of Bible study and a set devotional time, others promote solitude and contemplative prayer. Some churches place great value on liturgies and creeds, emphasising continuity with Christians through the ages, while others find something fresh and vital in highlighting new songs, new words and new sounds. For one tradition the high point of a service is found in Holy Communion, for another it is the sermon. One church stream may commit a lot of time to evangelism and social action, while another invests much more in spiritual renewal and refreshment. Some Christians make a point of active political engagement, while others avoid it at all costs, seeing it as a distraction from the work of the gospel.

STUCK IN A BOX

Most of the time, however, we don't get a chance to see this rich diversity of spiritual formation within the global Church, let alone experience it. And there is so much out there! Are we missing out on opportunities to connect with God in a wider range of authentic and dynamic ways? Our spiritual practices are largely shaped by the Christian traditions we've known, or with which we feel comfortable. These can be reassuring, but they can also become a box that we find it hard to break out of: instead of our practices being an expression of our walk with God, they become *the* way, the *only* way to grow in our relationship with God. We might even become a little critical of how other traditions do things. But what happens when our practices become overfamiliar or dull, when we are just going through the motions? Or what happens if we dare to admit to ourselves that it is simply not working? Your tradition may emphasise contemplative prayer – but you just can't do it. In fact you can't bear it; it sends you to sleep. Everybody else around you may seem to enjoy Bible study, but you can't get into it and you are bored. You might be left feeling frustrated and that you cannot connect with God. Or worse, you might end up thinking you're a failure and it's because you're not good enough or don't try hard enough. What began as a rich expression of your relationship with God has been reduced to a stifling uniformity to what you think you should do to be a good Christian. And it's not working. We're burned out on religion.

BREAK OUT OF THE BOX

You made all the delicate, inner parts of my body
    and knit me together in my mother's womb.
Thank you for making me so wonderfully complex!
    Your workmanship is marvellous – how well I know it.[1]

In the same way that our Church heritage is rich and diverse, so are we Christians. We're marvellously made, wonderfully complex, diverse, as God intended. We're of different colours and cultures; we have different interests, we've known different life experiences. We're simply different people. In the light of this, isn't it a bit odd to expect our spiritual practices to look the same, smell the same, taste the same and *be* the same as those of Christians around us? On one level it's obvious, yet it doesn't seem to stop us comparing ourselves with other Christians. We feel inadequate because we're not like the Christian spiritual giants we know. We conclude that this is the reason why we are not effective and why our lives resemble Ronald Sider's statistics. We are not good enough; and until we pray better/read the Bible better/witness more/save the world better, we never will be.

God took great delight in creating us, shaping us inside and out. There's something about our rich, unique design that He desires to connect with. After all, we were made for a relationship with Him. Yet if we are stuck in our boxes of how we perceive things *should* be done, our connection to God weakens. We cannot relate to Him in someone else's way, no matter how impressive. It's us He wants. We need to break out of the box and discover how we have been designed to relate to Him. One size does not fit all. There are lots of things that shape how we do life with God. We have different personalities, styles of learning, ways of expressing love, and we experience different phases of life. What do these different things bring to our spiritual practices?

DIFFERENT PERSONALITIES

Personality type assessments are a common feature in today's world. They're used to train teams in the workplace, to help couples in marriage counselling and to bring clarity in personal coaching or careers advice. Leading people through a series of questions or scenarios, these tools aim to help them gain a fuller picture of their personality and how they interact with others. The results chart behaviour patterns in times of stability or pressure, and help us and those around us understand who we are and why we act the way we do. While these tools cannot pick up every nuance of our culture and background, the awareness they do bring can strengthen a team's effectiveness, or bring needed insight into the workings of our significant relationships. An awareness of our personality can be incredibly valuable as we invest in our relationship with God.

For example, one big difference between people is whether they're introverted or extroverted.

Extroverts are energised by the world around them. They can spend time alone and enjoy it from time to time, but given the choice, their preference is to spend time with other people, because it is vibrant and stimulating and it's what they need, not because they are inherently insecure, but because it's how they were designed. They may have a wide network of relationships. Life is a shared experience, active and involved in lots of activities. They process their thoughts through conversation with other people, because they find it helpful to talk it out and hear what others have to say. It's simply how they are wonderfully made.

For extroverted Christians, interacting with people can have a huge role. Active group discussion can be incredibly stimulating for the extroverts' relationship with God, as they share with others what they are experiencing. They might find that some of the key moments in their life with God have come through conversations with other people. Church retreats or Christian conferences might be an ideal smorgasbord of experiences, but also the social side of things could be equally renewing. For extroverts, a spiritual life might be a particularly active one, where they enjoy being active and meeting lots of people along the way. And as well as feeling refreshed, the stimulation from interacting with new ideas and learning and engaging in conversations contributes something dynamic to life with God.

Yet for extroverts, extended times alone might become draining. The idea of a quiet time might feel very noble, but we might not feel very good at it, even a little intimidated. The idea of spending prolonged periods of time in silence, with no interaction or external stimulus, may feel unfocused at best, and at worst horrifying! Guiltily we may trudge through times of silence and solitude, wondering if there is more to spiritual depth and maturity than this.

Introverts operate in a different way. Introverts are not necessarily shy or insecure; they have quality relationships and social skills and can be perfectly happy in a social setting. It's just that their preference is to recharge alone. Introverts tend to prefer reflecting on thoughts and ideas on the inside. They like to process internally before sharing their considered ideas. Instead of a breadth of activities and experiences, they may prefer to focus on a few to a deeper level. Their internal world brings them to life and they need time alone in order to have something to give to the people and the world around them.

So for introverts, silence can be quite refreshing. It's a chance to be still away from the storms of life. The opportunity for retreat in silence and solitude could be a life-changing spiritual mountain-top experience. It could provide a God-given creative opportunity to listen and reflect on ideas. Back at home, a small, close and established community of friends can provide an environment to study the Word, pray or be activists together. Writing a journal might be another practice that introverts find useful. Yet at a big conference or festival, the sheer volume of people and experiences can present a challenge for introverts. At times like this, they might appreciate some time alone to recharge so that they are not completely drained by the very event that was supposed to refresh them!

These are just two well-known personality differences, but we can probably think of many more. Some people like to give structure to their lives. They like goals and order and a plan to work towards. Yet that would be anathema to people who prefer a more spontaneous go-with-the-flow approach to life. Their lives with God would look very different, but they're both made in God's image and He delights in who they are.

Q. Have you ever considered how your personality might shape how you do life with God and the spiritual practices that help or hinder your relationship with Him?

We could consider other differences, such as our learning styles. Some of us learn through language and words, while others take a more systematical, mathematical approach, exploring logic and patterns. Some educators contend that there may be up to eight learning styles.[2] For example, some people are visual learners, preferring images and other visual tools. For Christians who learn best visually, the use of art and images may enhance how they connect with God. Some have a physical learning style, using the body, sense of touch and physical activities to learn about the surrounding world. For Christians who learn physically, a quiet time might be more effective alongside activity, like a run, a hike or even gardening!

Q. How do you learn? And how could your learning style shape the practices you adopt to learn more about God?

DIFFERENT SEASONS OF LIFE

As we break out of our boxes to broaden our spiritual practices to connect with God in everyday life, there is one more area to consider. We don't just have these richly diverse personalities which shape and define us. Our lives are also shaped and defined by the reality of our stage of life.

In my university student days I enjoyed great freedom and flexibility. My Biblical Studies degree schedule was very laid back. I was expected to do a lot of reading . . . but let's just say I had a lot of spare time! I was free to immerse myself in my local church because my degree didn't have the same demands as my engineer and medic friends were facing. My summer holidays were fifteen weeks long. The space provided the opportunity to go to Christian festivals, on short-term mission trips, or sometimes just to a Greek island! I was zealous for God, I had the time, I had the energy and I was surrounded by lots of people in the same position. It was great. There were prayer meetings that lasted for hours, intense theological debates and long student gatherings. In those days, in that community, real God in real life seemed effortless.

I wasn't the only one who found the transition to the working world something of a shock! In this stage of life you might leave a thriving student church and Christian Union and turn up with a new job in a new city where you're the only Christian at work. Not only are you dealing with transitions, but perhaps you're also dealing with new challenges to your faith. What does it mean to be ethical, godly and holy in your environment? And where do you go with all your questions? There's a small group that starts at 7 p.m., but you get home from work at 7 p.m. and you're exhausted. It's too much effort to make for people you don't know. I lived with nurses, teachers and a computer programmer in my twenties. They were committed believers, but the nurses were dealing with night shifts and unsociable hours. The teachers came home and had more work to do. The programmer had these periods when he'd virtually have to live at work to meet deadlines. Somewhere in the midst of life they were trying to grow and mature in their walk with God, to be active at church. It was challenging.

Another shift happens as people enter serious relationships and begin to settle down. Emotionally there can be something of a change of allegiances, a shift in priorities. Some of us might acknowledge that our significant other seemed to take God's place for a while. We felt happy, and then possibly a little guilty if we talked to God more when we felt we needed Him more. We used to be more active in church life, but now we spend time visiting relatives, or IKEA, catching up after a crazy week at work. What does spirituality look like for a couple?

Then there's the season of a young family. We may be raising our children alone or with our spouse, but we're all tired! In the months after our daughter Tia was born, I tried hard to have some kind of quiet time. Yet every time I got out a Bible and sat down to read, I fell asleep. I had to change my expectations because I existed in a sleep-deprived haze. Never have I felt I needed God's help so much while feeling so incapable of being with Him, or concentrating on Him in any way. At that time mission trips and deep theological study were out of the question. I craved sleep, a bath, clothes that fitted and an adult conversation.

And as the girls grow, the fun continues. With each season of life, I've needed to explore new ways of investing in my relationship with God.

The different seasons of our lives present us with new challenges, new opportunities and new limitations. We may be dealing with chronic illness, or caring for a family member. We might have taken on a new job. The old practices don't always make the transition. If I looked back on my student days as the definitive way to be with God, I'd feel inadequate for years. I could try hard to relive the past, but I'd soon be burned out on religion. My life season has changed, my responsibilities have changed. Thankfully, my God remains the same. I just need to explore how to do life with God now.

Q. How does the season of life you're currently in influence the nature of your relationship with God?

TWO BIG CHALLENGES WE HAVE IN COMMON

It's incredibly releasing to explore the diversity of a life with God. It brings vigour and life to us, and we'll return to the subject in more detail in later chapters. However, while it is an important piece in understanding a real relationship with God, it is not the full picture. Sider's statistics and the Church's decline cannot be explained simply by a lack of creativity in spiritual practices. There's more to the story. We need to look at two issues that run far deeper and that shape the Christians we become. If we don't attend to them, our faith is fundamentally weakened. But if we engage with them, there is the potential for transformation.

The first is the issue of the *human heart*.

In biblical terms, the heart refers to much more than our emotions or dreams. In both the Old and New Testaments the 'heart' also encompasses our thoughts, our will, our decisions and choices. It's the centre of our passions and our appetites; it's our physical and spiritual core. It's no surprise, then, that the Bible says, 'Above all else, guard your heart, for everything you do flows from it.'[3]

In Mark 7, the religious leaders confront Jesus because He and some disciples ate without undertaking a ritual hand-washing before the meal. It was an affront to religious tradition and, according to the religious leaders, made them 'unclean'. Jesus used this exchange to explain to the crowds and the disciples that the many external rules that religious leaders used to define people as 'clean' or 'unclean' were inaccurate. It wasn't about public religious behaviour; it was about the heart.

He went on: 'What comes out of you is what defiles you. For from within, out of your hearts, come evil thoughts, sexual immorality, theft, murder, adultery, greed, malice, deceit, lewdness, envy, slander, arrogance and folly. All these evils come from inside and defile you.'[4]

The list of issues I read about in the library on that day bear striking similarities to the list that Jesus describes here. It is not about whether we are 'good' or 'bad' Christians – it has always been about the state of our hearts. We knew our hearts needed help when we first responded to the message of the gospel. We knew that our hearts needed a Saviour. However, surrendering our heart to Jesus is not a one-off event. There are new thoughts that fill our hearts as we go through life; new battles of the will. There are new attitudes and appetites that demand our attention: a fleeting sexual attraction to someone other than our spouse, a hunger for power that insists it be satisfied. We may have experienced things that have left huge wounds in our hearts: a harrowing divorce, a betrayal of some kind.

The religious leaders accusing Jesus thought religious traditions and practices were what was important, and missed the Son of God standing before them. If, like them, we do not pay attention to the condition of our hearts, we find ourselves in the same position. This is true for all of us, regardless of culture, personality or life stage. If we want a life-transforming relationship with God, then our hearts matter.

CHANGED HEARTS

I was reminded of how God can change the human heart after church one Sunday night. I'd just finished preaching and was looking for my friends to get a lift home, when a middle-aged man approached me.

'Excuse me. Can I talk to you for a minute?'

'Sure,' I replied, looking for my friends all the more keenly. It was late; I was tired and hoped this wasn't going to be a long conversation. Then I noticed that the man actually seemed quite nervous. He looked at the ground and spoke quickly.

'I'm forty-seven years old, and all my life I have been a racist.'

He paused. I stared at him, finally giving him my undivided attention. I had flashbacks of the times I'd been mocked, verbally abused, spat at and judged for the colour of my skin. I said nothing, but the hurt, anger and disbelief were all in my eyes. My heart raced as I wondered what he was waiting for. The tension was palpable. In that moment there was no one else in the room, just a tall white man and a tall black woman facing one another.

He took a deep breath and continued. 'When you stood up to preach tonight, the Lord showed me the hatred in my heart. He told me it was sinful, and I've repented. So I just wanted to tell you and to thank you for speaking, to thank you for your ministry. The Lord has changed my heart today and He's set me free.' He reached out his hand to shake mine.

The tension was broken. I was stunned. All I could manage was, 'Thank you. Thank you.' I smiled, my hand met his, we shook hands and he left.

I was quiet on the way home that night, still reeling from this man's words, from his honesty, vulnerability and the risk he took, the conviction in his spirit. For a while I couldn't place how I felt. It was an amazing conversation. But it was much more than that, it was strangely liberating. That night God had changed my heart too; it was healing.

I wonder how your heart is today. Perhaps it's diseased with pride or greed, or broken by circumstances or disappointment. What could change in your life if God transformed your heart? Would it save your marriage, end an illicit relationship? Would it address the anger that explodes inside you?

JESUS – ARE YOU A FAN OR A FOLLOWER?

The second issue we all have in common concerns how we approach our *relationship with Jesus*. My husband Chris and I both love football. Or at least, that is how I see it. He has a different idea.

He would say that I'm a *fan* of football teams, but he's a *follower*, and apparently they are *not* the same!

So what does life as a fan look like? I love football, especially when my teams (yes, I intentionally wrote *teams*) are winning. And if they start losing, I simply choose another one that is winning. That way I am never disappointed. I know I'm a fair-weather fan, there for the good times. Some would be so blunt as to call me a glory-hunter, saying that all I care about are the accolades and the pride that comes with being successful, the opportunity to look down on the losing side. And they would be right. Chris, however, has a lifelong allegiance to one team. He is faithful, no matter what it takes. Wherever he is in the world, whatever the time difference, he will sacrifice sleep if necessary and get up at ridiculous times of the night if it means he can watch his team play (I only do that for the England games, for Nigeria, and sometimes for Brazil. Otherwise I'm happy to find out the result when I wake up). He reads about his team daily, he cares deeply about players and their injuries and the manager and the transfer market. He knows all about them. I simply don't have the time or energy to care about all my teams. When Chris's team wins he is elated, and when they lose he suffers (we all do). But nothing will change his commitment to his team. Nothing. Not ever. I can follow for a while, under favourable circumstances. He will follow his team for life.

Whether you're a fan or a follower when it comes to football isn't a big deal (at least not to me), but if we use those descriptions to illustrate how we relate to Jesus, it's another matter. Are you a fan of Jesus or a follower? Fans love Jesus, and they appreciate all He does. But they can be distracted by all the other exciting alternatives to actually following Him, like living for themselves or others. It's not necessarily a shallow faith, but it is a conditional commitment, love and life on their own terms.

Followers respond to Jesus' words, 'Follow me.'[5] They understand that to *follow* Jesus means to leave the road they're on and unite themselves to His road.[6] They know that they now walk His way. They don't just believe what He did is important; they understand that Jesus came down to our world and modelled how to do life with God. So they seek to apply His principles and imitate His practices in their lives. If Jesus has principles about forgiveness (which He does), then they become His followers' principles too. If Jesus practises active compassion to the outcast and the broken, then His followers find ways to practise that too. Sometimes it's amazing. Sometimes it's incredibly difficult and costly, just as it was for Jesus. But while fans may change allegiances at this point, followers are still there, following Jesus' example.

In my years at St Thomas's Church in Sheffield, our vicar Mike Breen developed Life Shapes, a series of discipleship tools illustrated by shapes. Each shape focused on an aspect of how Jesus lived and how to follow His example. Using a triangle as an illustration, Mike observed that Jesus lived out three main priorities in his life:

- **Up**wards – Jesus had a close relationship to the Father.
- **In**wards – Jesus had meaningful relationships with other believers.
- **Out**wards – Jesus was the good news and shared it with the world around Him, a combination of evangelism and service.[7]

Jesus defined for us what true spirituality actually looked like as He walked on earth. We'll explore these three priorities that Jesus demonstrated in the second section of the book, 'Practising Life'. In the meantime, there's a fundamental question that needs to be answered.

Q. Are you a fan or a follower?

THE INCREDIBLE CHALLENGE

Like the Christians who have gone before us and now stand as 'a cloud of witnesses', we too need to respond to the challenges of our culture, cultivating a real and dynamic faith. We can respond to the challenges, recorded in statistics, seen in our communities, seen in our hearts, in a more tangible way than crying out loud in a library. We can respond by giving God constant access to our hearts, the very centre of our lives. We can respond by embracing Jesus not just as fair-weather fans, but as followers modelling our lives after Him.

It's an incredible challenge; we can already tell it's not going to be easy. Trying harder won't cut it; we'll need to train.

2

In training

Have nothing to do with godless myths and old wives' tales; rather, train yourself to be godly. For physical training is of some value, but godliness has value for all things, holding promise for both the present life and the life to come.
(1 Timothy 4:7–8)

Spiritual transformation is not a matter of trying hard, but of training wisely.
(John Ortberg)[1]

'TAKE MY YOKE UPON YOU AND LEARN FROM ME'[2]

It was 6.30 a.m. and I was standing outside my house, eager and ready to go. I'd enrolled in the Race For Life, a 5 km run organised by Cancer Research UK, and this was my first day of training. It was a brilliant opportunity to support a wonderful cause and get fitter. I'd been athletic in my secondary school years, so this wasn't going to be a problem. I'd even bought a new outfit to get me in the right frame of mind. I was feeling good about this run. I took a deep breath and confidently took to the streets.

It was at this point that I discovered that training was amazing for my prayer life. Within less than two minutes I was crying out to God on my knees, wheezing, '*God, save me!*' My athletic history, my great new outfit, my shiny new trainers could not help me now. I was unfit and I couldn't breathe. It was a disaster. Still, I'd told everyone I'd entered for this fundraising run. I couldn't back out.

So I began to train. The next few weeks were humbling as I slowly learned how to put one foot in front of another quickly while breathing. There were many mornings when I woke up dreading the idea of going for a run. The bed was so warm and comfortable – why leave it? Perhaps I needed sleep. It was raining outside; I couldn't possibly run in those conditions, could I? My hair would get wet. I still ached from the last run. What if I got an injury or something? Maybe I'll be late for work, maybe I should get some breakfast . . . the excuses were endless. One of our friends lived on my running route, so occasionally I'd find myself stopping outside their house – you know, just to say 'hi'. It would be rude to say 'no' to the offer of a coffee, a croissant, a bacon sandwich, wouldn't it? When I did actually run, my mind cried out in resistance, telling me I'd never make it, it was a bad idea and I was a fool for trying. Or it would tell me that the cause I was running for was no big deal, and perhaps I could support it in a less painful way. Sponsor someone else, give them £10 and leave it at that. My body just seemed to beg me to stop. The days when I fell in the street in front of people were particularly special; I tried to make out somehow that I'd absolutely intended to kiss the pavement and acquire extensive bruising. Still nothing could take away the abject humiliation I felt. In time I got better. It even hurt less. By the time the race took place, I was hooked. I kept on running. I learned different training exercises to improve. Most of the time, though, I didn't feel that I was achieving very much. As far as I could tell, all I did was run around the community looking a mess and trying not to fall down.

Months later my husband and I decided to go for a run, just for the fun of it, around a lake. By the end of it I was almost in tears, my body racked in pain, crying out those familiar words, '*God, save me!*' Only this time it was two hours later, not two minutes. I didn't know it in that moment, but I'd just done a half-marathon.

TRAIN YOURSELF TO BE GODLY

The New Testament includes two letters that the apostle Paul writes to Timothy. Timothy is a young man who was converted in his teens through Paul's ministry, and eventually he joins Paul's missionary team. They enjoy a close relationship; Paul often describes Timothy as his son. Paul writes these letters when Timothy is based at the church in Ephesus. His letters are packed with a combination of advice concerning the Ephesian community and about Timothy's own personal growth. In his first letter Paul says that in the pressured times that the church is facing, many will opt out of following Jesus, enticed away by deceptive ideas. He calls Timothy to point this out to the church community, then he speaks directly into Timothy's life.

Paul understood that any Christian can be drawn away into godless values and habits, even committed leaders like Timothy. Paul saw that what was needed was both a distancing from those values, but also an active pursuit of a different approach and focus. He called for a life of training in godliness. *The Message* translation of the text describes it this way:

> Stay clear of silly stories that get dressed up as religion. Exercise daily in God – no spiritual flabbiness, please! Workouts in the gymnasium are useful, but a disciplined life in God is far more so, making you fit both today and forever.[3]

We have already acknowledged at the start of this book that, like the Ephesian community, we buy into godless values and habits, perhaps unaware of the consequences. We try hard to be better.

Paul's advice to Timothy offers a powerful insight into how we engage with the state of our hearts and learn to follow Jesus.

Training to be godly is not purely about moral behaviour. There are plenty of people who aren't Christians who live inspirational lives. Godliness involves having a close relationship with God, so much so that His character is seen in our character, His life in our life. They are completely interconnected. *Our hearts are totally connected to and surrendered to His gracious love and mighty power; producing the life of a follower.* That's what we're training in.

TRAINING IS . . .

Do you remember the last time you had to train for something? Maybe it was the endless monotony of doing your scales on the piano. You were told they were essential, but you weren't convinced. Or perhaps it was exam revision, stumbling over that section that refused to sink in. Do you remember your first driving lesson? It was going so well until that manoeuvre that nearly caused a collision and got everybody's horns going. Perhaps you remember the drama of potty training your kids, wondering if it would ever come together, or if your child would be the only eleven-year-old in nappies at their school. Perhaps your training memories revolve around a team activity: training was hard work, but also produced a team camaraderie.

'Train yourself to be godly' is a statement that's both intimidating and reassuring.

It's intimidating because to train *yourself* to be godly denotes a level of personal responsibility. Our godliness is not simply determined by the sound teaching or the worship at our church. Since we train ourselves, we don't get to be passive consumers of Christian belief. We don't get to be victims here. We're going to have to work at it a little, maybe even a lot. We're not training to earn God's love and acceptance. We work hard at our significant relationships because we love the people involved, not because we want to earn their love. Similarly, we're investing in our relationship with God because we love Him and believe it's a relationship worth working at. Dallas Willard explains it brilliantly: 'Grace is not opposed to effort, it is opposed to earning. Earning is an attitude. Effort is an action.'[4]

It's also intimidating because we know from our personal experiences that training can be hard work. It can be dull, stretching, tiring, disheartening. It can even be painful. We've come to accept this in learning an instrument, passing an exam, preparing for a new career, but we may find it harder in our relationship with God. Our world has found many ways to create shortcuts for the things we want. We buy fast food or use a microwave to get food quickly. There's speed dating, a way to meet as many people as possible in the short time that life allows. We own phones that have so many applications that they enable us to listen to music, surf the Web, get directions, find a good restaurant. But even our busy culture acknowledges that success is not instantaneous. A closer look at the lives of the great athletes, artists and businessmen and women of our culture reveals that behind the fame, accolades and wealth is the story of training, sacrifice and sometimes loneliness in order to reach their goal. A mature relationship with God is not acquired instantly. It will require training.

Still, the call to godliness training is also a reassuring one. Training gives us permission to be a work in progress, liberating us from the unrealistic expectation of instant achievement. We're allowed to practise in order to improve. We expect training to be slow, to have good days when it all miraculously comes together and bad days when it all disastrously falls apart. We expect it to be frustrating and know that we won't always look good. We anticipate that not everyone will go at the same pace, but that's OK. We know that training can be creative; we practise those guitar chords and it inspires a song. Training is a springboard for new ideas. And if we keep at it, even when it looks as if we're getting nowhere, training can be incredibly effective.

When we apply the same principles to our relationship with God, as the Bible suggests, it makes it so much more accessible. Jesus invites us to 'learn from' Him.[5] He calls His followers 'disciples'. The word we find in the New Testament for 'disciples' is *mathetes*, meaning 'student', or 'learner'. It's not only OK for us to learn; Jesus describes His future followers that way in the Great Commission.[6] It redefines our expectations and opens up new opportunities. We're in training. So perhaps it will take a while to surrender our hearts fully to God, but we can practise that principle. We'll know, when it's hard and stretching, that this is what training looks like and we don't need to give up. We may not feel we've got all three elements of life as a follower in place, but we can learn them, we can practise them and we can grow. When it's dull and repetitive, we'll know not to be discouraged; this is what training looks like. But we'll also keep our eyes open for any creative opportunities that may arise. And we know that even if we can't see it straight away, our practising, our training, is making a powerful impact on our relationship with God. We don't have to be brilliant. We just have to keep running.

So where do we go from here? Do we embrace our unique personality and stage of life, choose habits that we like and feel comfortable with and just practise those? Not quite. Just as I was getting comfortable with my early morning run, my husband came out running with me and said he'd teach me to do to a fartlek.

DO A FARTLEK!

Er . . . *what*? I know the name sounds bizarre, but once you get past the giggling, I promise you it's a brilliant concept! Fartlek derives its name from a Swedish term meaning 'speed play'. It was made famous in the 1930s by a Swedish coach called Gøsta Holmér, who developed the method for his cross-country team. Today it's a technique used in training in many sports. In the course of a run, you select a landmark in the distance and pick up the pace and run hard at it. When you reach the target, you return to your ordinary pace until you recover. Then you pick another target in the distance, and the process continues.

When I did my first fartlek, I thought that if I ever lived to get home, I might kill my husband for this training session, or at least ask him what I had done so wrong to deserve such a punishment! But Chris knew what he was doing. In time, these short bursts of agony began to raise my overall fitness and ability. Now, I still can't say I love them, but I know they are powerful! A more structured approach is interval training. Interval training intersperses high-intensity workouts with times or intervals of rest or low activity.

Perhaps we'll leave some of the names behind, but these are great ideas to apply to our godliness training. There are some spiritual practices that come naturally to me. I love times of sung worship, the bigger and louder the better. It's comfortable for me, I meet God there and catch a glimpse of heaven. But if that's all I did, I'd be missing out and I would have an unbalanced picture of following Jesus. A short burst of fasting, or silence, may feel like agony and be particularly hard work for my personality. I'm stretched, hungry and lonely – but the different things I learn about God in the fast, in the silence, mature my walk with God. When I'm back singing in the crowd, my worship has an added depth. Those other practices have helped me know God better. The practices that don't come naturally to us are still incredibly important to our relationship with God, no matter how unnatural they may feel. We've all done uncomfortable things for the people we love. My daughter's first dance recital included the 'Daddy and Daughter' dance, when all the dads did a 'Greased Lightning' and hip-hop combo with their children in front of hundreds of people. I promise you there was not a dancer among them! But they undertook weeks of dance classes and discomfort because they loved their kids. We invest in the practices we enjoy because we love the dynamism that comes with being ourselves with God. It's a great connection. We invest in the practices that don't come naturally to us because we love God. It's a different connection, but still a great one.

From the interval training we can learn the idea of rotating a variety of practices in our lives. We can also apply the illustration to recognise that in certain seasons of life we might be particularly active, like in a high-intensity workout. But another season, for example when we first have young children, or when we experience loss and bereavement, might result in different practices. We simply cannot maintain the intensity of a previous season. But instead of drifting into guilt, we can embrace and value different practices that recognise where we're at. Our growth and maturity may look unfamiliar. For example, when I'm interval training, it takes me a while to recognise the value of the rest periods. Can I really be getting fitter by doing less, or even nothing? Surely I need to be active! But the growth is still there. The same is true for us as we engage in those slower seasons. The growth is still there; it just looks different. We may only recognise it in hindsight.

OUR TRAINING PROGRAMME

Personal trainers and fitness experts maintain that it's important to vary an exercise programme with strength, cardio and stretching exercises. The variety is good for our overall fitness and the body doesn't just get used to the one form of exercise, lessening its impact. Perhaps the best way to see the rest of this book is as two complementary parts of one training programme. They address different things, but they work well together.

Section One: Heart Practices

Section One addresses what is happening on the inside as we pursue our relationship with God. The unresolved issues in our hearts hurt and even restrict us. They define our relationship with God and with the people around us. We can't change ourselves, but it doesn't have to end there. God offers us salvation, healing and freedom; His power can transform our lives. This section suggests some practices we can follow that give God greater access to our hearts.

Section Two: Practising Life

Section Two looks at practices that help us grow as followers. Imitating the pattern of Jesus, they address the three priorities we see at work in His life.

- **Up** – attend to a relationship with God the Father.
- **In** – attend to relationships with other believers.
- **Out** – attend to our relationship with the world around us.[7]

We might find we are strong in one or two of these areas. This section offers us encouragement and ideas for both the areas of strength and the areas of weakness. Some of the practices are hundreds of years old, drawing on the experiences of global Christians in Church history. Some ideas are more contemporary, where Christians share how they walk with God in today's culture. There are some practices that will appeal to the extrovert, others to the introvert. There are practices that will appeal in different phases of life. Take note of the particular practices that help you give God access to your heart. Invite Him to meet your there with the unlimited resources of His grace and power. In the range of spiritual traditions represented, some may fit naturally. Some will be a springboard for other creative ideas. Enjoy the variety and develop your own training programme! The common thread is that these practices are tools that help us meet with Jesus in everyday life. Life with Jesus is our goal and it's Him we're living for.

So, are you ready to train yourself to be godly?

> Therefore, since we are surrounded by such a great cloud of witnesses, let us throw off everything that hinders and the sin that so easily entangles. And let us run with perseverance the race marked out for us, fixing our eyes on Jesus, the pioneer and perfecter of faith. For the joy that was set before him he endured the cross, scorning its shame, and sat down at the right hand of the throne of God. Consider him who endured such opposition from sinners, so that you will not grow weary and lose heart.[8]

Let's start running.

SECTION ONE
Heart Practices

3

Practising surrender

Then he called the crowd to him along with his disciples and said: 'Whoever wants to be my disciple must deny themselves and take up their cross and follow me. For whoever wants to save their life will lose it, but whoever loses their life for me and for the gospel will save it. What good is it for you to gain the whole world, yet forfeit your soul?'
(Mark 8:34–6)

Therefore, I urge you, brothers and sisters, in view of God's mercy, to offer your bodies as a living sacrifice, holy and pleasing to God – this is true worship.
(Romans 12:1)

The greatness of a man's power is the measure of his surrender.
(William Booth, Founder of the Salvation Army)

'So how can I help you?'

I was finally sitting in the doctor's office. For years I'd experienced pain and wheezing when I ran, but assumed it was simply because I was unfit. I was used to it and just compensated where necessary. Then one day I decided to have a check-up. After asking a few questions and assessing the situation, my doctor told me I had 'restrictive airways disease' and prescribed an inhaler for me. 'See if it makes a difference,' he said.

The following day I used my medicine before a run. Did it

make a difference? It made a huge difference! I'd thought that I was just unfit; I didn't know that I wasn't well. I'd been compensating for years; I'd simply adjusted my expectations. I was able to work out when the pain would come, so I held back. Now I was disorientated. Could things have been different? Perhaps I wouldn't have been so hard on myself for not being able to run as well I thought I could. I wondered if I'd ever put myself in danger out of ignorance: could I have had an asthma attack? I felt freer than ever before. I had room to breathe that I simply didn't know was there. I could run faster, longer. Running would be different from now on.

Our heart issues function a bit like restrictive airways disease. They limit our ability and desire to run the race marked out for us. We could have everything else in place, but if our hearts aren't free and whole, our relationship with God is restricted. Our lives are affected as borkenness seeps into our thoughts and feelings, our habits and choices and our relationships. The good news is that God reaches out with power and mercy to heal and restore broken lives. We can't fix ourselves; we need Him. So we need to get into the habit of regularly giving God access to our hearts. This section suggests four practices to help us with that. We'll start with practising surrender.

GREAT EXPECTATIONS

When you became a Christian, what did you sign up for?

When we first met Jesus He was described to us in a number of ways: Saviour, Friend, Healer, Father, Lord, King. We were given a number of descriptions of what being a Christian would mean. We were told that our eternal destiny was now resolved, we'd been rescued by a powerful king. In everyday life we now had someone watching over us, a Father whom we could talk to, who looked out for us and provided for us. All we needed to do was raise a hand, repeat a prayer.

And what were we to do with the rest of our lives? Some of us were told that He knew our every need and want and desire. He would take care of everything because He had the power to do so. Some were told that being a Christian was an integral part of their national identity. Being a Christian meant being a good citizen, abiding by the laws of the land. For some, Christianity meant being good, giving to charity and helping people in need. To others it meant leaving a culture behind. A new wardrobe was required. They no longer attended certain places, saw particular people – in case they were negatively influenced. They had new friends, a new family now.

But did anyone tell you that you had chosen to die?

These ideas all represent aspects of the Christian life, but sometimes we can leave out of the picture the full extent of what a relationship with God means. Jesus is our Saviour, Friend and King. He is the Healer. His sacrifice has made the way for us to know our heavenly Father! Knowing God involves both awe and reverence *and* friendship and intimacy: what an incredible gift! Furthermore, it's important that what we believe is reflected in how we live our daily life. Being a Christian will affect who we are in the community, how we relate to those in need. It is vital that we make decisions on how we express our values.

But again, did anyone tell you that you had chosen to die?

Mark's Gospel is intense and action packed, and chapter 8 is no exception. The chapter opens with the miracle of Jesus feeding a crowd of four thousand men (and potentially their families) who have been travelling with Him for three days. After everyone is fed, Jesus and the disciples head out on a boat to the Dalmanutha region. There, Jesus warns the disciples of the impact of the religious leaders' teachings. When they reach Bethsaida, Jesus heals a blind man. As they continue on their mission through the villages, Peter gets it. He gets who Jesus is, he understands how significant Jesus is – that He is the Messiah. And he blurts it out. But then Jesus explains what that means. It's a path of sacrifice and death and then, finally, resurrection. Peter can't handle Jesus' words. This is not a description of the Messiah that people had longed for, for generations. How could this Messiah liberate the people from Roman occupation and years of oppression through *suffering and death*? That is not how God intended it to be! In protest, Peter takes Jesus aside to straighten out His theology. I'm sure that Peter was as shocked as we are by Jesus' response:

> 'Get behind me, Satan!' he said. 'You do not have in mind the concerns of God, but merely human concerns.'[1]

Jesus calls the disciples and the crowds closer to Him. This is something they all need to hear and understand. This is not just Peter's embarrassing moment; he may just have had the misfortune to blurt out loud what others were thinking. What Jesus had to say, though, was not just for the committed believers, or for the missionary types who had left their professions to follow Jesus and join His team. It was for every member of the crowd, young and old, men, women and children. Everyone needed to understand what it really meant to follow Him.

> Then he called the crowd to him along with his disciples and said: 'Whoever wants to be my disciple must deny themselves and take up their cross and follow me.'[2]

SCANDALOUS SACRIFICE

These words were absolutely scandalous! For twenty-first-century readers, the cross is a symbol of the Christian faith. For Christians it's the source of our salvation. We get the rest of the story. But in that moment, the crowd and the disciples were just invited to pick up an instrument of humiliation, torture and persecution, the symbol of an evil criminal's death. This image was a scandal to the culture, an offence. Yet that was the imagery, the symbol Jesus chose to use to describe what it meant to follow Him. He told them that following Him means self-denial. Self-denial means *not* getting what you want, *not* coming first, and carrying a cross instead. As if to drive the message home, He continues:

> For whoever wants to save their life will lose it, but whoever loses their life for me and for the gospel will save it.[3]

The Greek word translated 'life' here, *psuche*, is worth close examination. *Psuche* doesn't just refer to your everyday activities in life. *Psuche* can also refer to your interior life, your soul, your desires, your will, your mind. Does that sound familiar? *Psuche* carries similar nuances to the biblical understanding of *the heart*. When Jesus talked to that crowd, He invited them to surrender their hearts and lives to follow Him. Life no longer happened on their terms. Surrender was not a one-off event – it was a life of daily self-denial.[4] It might cost them their physical lives. If not, it would cost them their lives in every other way – their will, desires, mind, their very core, their heart. It was a call to choose to surrender – to put to death – everything, and in doing so to receive the kind of life that only Jesus can give. It was a call to scandalous sacrifice.

That's what Jesus called people to when He said, 'Come, follow me.'[5] That is what they signed up for. That is what *we* signed up for.

SURRENDER IN AN AGE OF ENTITLEMENT

Jesus' words are radically and painfully challenging to us today.

43

Far removed from the self-help mantras, talk shows and gurus who encourage us to live for ourselves, Jesus' words leave no room for a self-centred life. He calls for surrender in an age of entitlement. His call to a life of daily self-denial is difficult to bear. His words strike at the heart of our egotistical moments and fantasies. Sometimes we believe that a life with Jesus means our desires are met on our terms. We craft Jesus into the god of our lives that we prefer Him to be: of course He'll do things our way; He loves us and longs to bless us. Harder still, Jesus' words also pose a challenge to the good things we want and long for. There is nothing wrong with wanting to get married, to get that promotion, to have a child. There is nothing wrong with wanting the best for our family. But can we surrender those things to God?

As if these words were not challenging enough, they come with a warning. When we try to retain control of our hearts and lives, we face ruining the very things we are holding onto. The CEV translates Jesus' words like this:

> If you want to save your life, you will destroy it. But if you give up your life for me and for the good news, you will save it. What will you gain, if you own the whole world but destroy yourself? What could you give to get back your soul?[6]

Throughout Church history, Christians have dealt with the implications of a surrendered life. Dietrich Bonhoeffer was a German Lutheran pastor and theologian during the rise of Hitler and the Third Reich. While many Christians promoted Nazi ideals as compatible with Christianity, or failed to denounce Nazism, Bonhoeffer was among those who consistently spoke out against the Third Reich in the 1930s. Banned from lecturing, he developed an underground seminary for pastors. In 1937, as Nazi persecution intensified, Bonhoeffer wrote *The Cost of Discipleship*, explaining:

> When Christ calls a man, he bids him come and die. It may be
> a death like that of the first disciples who had to leave home
> and work to follow him, or it may be a death like Luther's who
> had to leave the monastery and go out into the world. But it is
> the same death every time – death in Jesus Christ.[7]

In spite of increased pressure from the Nazis, Bonhoeffer continued to work underground with the church and joined the German resistance. In 1943 he was arrested and imprisoned. During his imprisonment, documents were discovered linking Bonhoeffer with a failed assassination attempt against Hitler. He was executed on 9 April 1945, mere weeks before Nazi Germany fell. A life fully surrendered cost Bonhoeffer his earthly life. Yet his works and his example lived on, teaching and influencing Christians for generations to follow.

LEARNING TO SURRENDER

In the twenty-first century the call continues. Surrender your heart and life: your desires, motives, will, goals, plans, choices, lifestyle. Pick up your cross daily; come and die. It's a call so bold that sometimes, like Peter, we too want to take Jesus to one side and point out His misguided theology.

Sometimes surrender is a one-off event. For example, we turn down a job offer we'd like, because we sense God indicating that it will be too disruptive to our family life and will undermine our priorities. It's a sacrifice to let it go; the job offer boosted our confidence. Still, we know it's the right thing, so we walk away.

Yet there are many situations where we need to keep surrendering, to carry our crosses daily.

I found that in certain areas of my life, surrender was a principle that required a lot of practice. I was so used to doing it my way, so convinced that I was entitled to live on my terms. Singleness was definitely one of those areas. I picked up my cross slowly, intermittently, accompanied by tears.

I was part of a fun, vibrant, passionate church, full of young adults. The worship was amazing, the teaching phenomenal. With such a large young adult community, eventually people started dating. Then engagements were announced, followed by weddings. Initially it was great fun, dressing up and singing at weddings. But after a while there came a point when I wanted it to be my turn and it just wasn't happening for me. I felt marriage was something I was called to, something that God had for me, so what was His problem?

At first it was unsettling, then annoying. Eventually it was just painful and I was lonely and frustrated. It was as though God had remembered everyone but me! I could handle the wedding days with dignity because I was celebrating my friends (and a new outfit didn't hurt either). Still, there were many sad and lonely days. I'd cry alone in my room at night, finally giving the bitterness and disappointment the chance to come out.

Surrender was difficult. There was a lot to surrender! Was Jesus more important than my request for a husband? Then surrender. Could I give Jesus my longings? My dreams had become my rights. Could I let them go, walk away from them, execute them? Surrender.

Could I surrender the disappointment that was slowly but surely infecting my theology, my understanding of God's wisdom, lordship and love?

Could I surrender the way I'd worshipped getting married, and put it before my God?

Could I daily surrender every part of my single life, even the growing desire to take matters into my own hands?

This was not a training programme that I thought I'd signed up for – not knowingly. But with hindsight I know those years were formative for me. In those moments I began to practise surrender.

It was essential for me to remind myself that surrender was a response to God's love, not a key to unlock the gates to God's approval, or the coin in the slot machine to release the heavenly jackpot of my answered prayer. It was the response to the amazing love I had first received, the response of a follower. The apostle Paul communicates something of this in the book of Romans. Chapter 11 closes in an incredible doxology as Paul breaks out of his thoughts and bursts into praise for just how phenomenal God is. Then, as if to respond to this revelation of God's greatness, he writes:

> Therefore, I urge you, brothers and sisters, in view of God's mercy, to offer your bodies as a living sacrifice, holy and pleasing to God – this is your true worship. Do not conform to the pattern of this world, but be transformed by the renewing of your mind. Then you will be able to test and approve what God's will is – his good, pleasing and perfect will.[8]

In view of God's mercy, we surrender. Paul's words conjure up the picture of living under the shadow of a cross. We look up, but can't see, blinded by the brilliance and radiance of God. And then we look down and see this shadow – of a cross, the symbol of mercy and grace. In view of God's mercy, we offer our bodies and appetites as a lifestyle of sacrifice. In view of God's mercy, we choose to pursue God's priorities and values, even if they clash with the world around us. In view of God's mercy, we invite God to transform our thoughts, our opinions, our very core, our *psuche*, our heart and our life. We take up our cross and nail to it what we need to surrender, and we follow wherever Jesus leads. On the cross it's no longer our own, it's no longer alive. We've walked away.

It's just not always that easy. Sometimes it's devastating.

FROM DEATH TO LIFE

I was delighted when I discovered I was pregnant for the second time. This baby was loved from the outset. I carried the news silently for a day just to revel in God's blessing. When I shared the news with my husband Chris the following evening, he was as overjoyed as I was.

It was all about to change.

The next day I woke up bleeding, and it wouldn't stop. I was terrified, and lay on my bed crying out to God as Chris called the doctor. The day was filled with medical appointments. A doctor gently told us how common miscarriages were, while I stared ahead, huge tears rolling down my face. There were tests to check my hormone levels, prescriptions to push the levels up. Then there was an ultrasound, during which the technician could not have sounded crueller when he said, 'I don't know why they even brought you here. There's nothing there, it's just a sack.' I hid from him in the bathroom.

I called friends, sobbing down the phone to their prayers and comforting words. I was bewildered and frightened and wanted to fight for my child and didn't know how. I'd never felt so out of control. All the while, my firstborn – still a baby herself – needed me too. By the end of the day we'd received the results of all the tests from the doctor's office. They were all inconclusive. It didn't look good, but they just didn't know; only time would tell.

It was Maundy Thursday of Holy Week. That evening there was a church service, and I felt compelled to be there. I slipped in quietly at the back. The room was in darkness, a solitary light resting on a wooden cross. It was an evening for meditation. The service walked through the last hours Jesus spent with His disciples, the last supper, the betrayal, Gethsemane.

There was a response time offered to the congregation. To symbolise Jesus carrying our sins on the cross, we were invited to write down the things that burdened us, our struggles and failures, and walk up to the cross. At the foot of the cross were nails and hammers waiting for us to nail our burdens to the cross and walk away free.

The congregation began to file forward, some joyfully nailing pieces of paper to the cross and walking away free. For me, amid the tests, technicians and doctors, the day was punctuated with desperate whispers or wails of 'Please, God, no . . .' but not much else. I didn't want to listen. I didn't want to know. I just wanted Him to hear me and do as I asked. He didn't need to speak. In that moment I didn't need a vision or a verse of Scripture. The wooden cross spoke loudly enough. It was time to surrender my baby, my longings for the prayer answer I wanted, everything. It was time to pick up my cross. On a piece of paper I wrote 'My Baby', and folded it gently into my hand.

Walking towards the cross was the loneliest walk of my life and it felt like the longest. I avoided the light shining on the cross for as long as I could, remaining in the shadows, letting people take their turn before me, but I still reached it. I got on my knees, blinded by my tears, fighting against letting go, surrendering again. The hammer and nail were so cold, and nailing that piece of paper to the cross was desperate. I mouthed silent prayers, whispered broken dreams. People continued to nail their own pieces of paper and walk away, but I wouldn't move. My baby was there. I couldn't. I knew I had to stand up and walk away, but how could I leave my baby? In the end, the only reason I could leave my baby there was because Jesus was there too. Stroking the piece of paper one last time, I said goodbye. Reluctantly I returned to the shadows where the prayer team now stood, and a friend prayed with me. I left the room utterly desolate, and drove away into the night.

All we could do was wait.

An ultrasound a few weeks later revealed a heartbeat, and a picture of a little someone wriggling around. I wailed.

At 1.38 p.m. on 9 December 2006, I held her in my arms, our precious newborn daughter. We named her Zoë, the word you find in the New Testament for 'life', the kind of life that comes only from God.

Q. Do you need to practise surrender?

> I am no longer my own but yours.
> Put me to what you will,
> rank me with whom you will;
> put me to doing,
> put me to suffering;
> let me be employed for you,
> or laid aside for you,
> exalted for you,
> or brought low for you;
> let me be full,
> let me be empty,
> let me have all things,
> let me have nothing:
> I freely and wholeheartedly yield all things
> to your pleasure and disposal.
> And now, glorious and blessed God,
> Father, Son and Holy Spirit,
> you are mine and I am yours.[9]

Take it to the cross and surrender. In view of God's mercy . . . surrender.

4
Practising forgiveness

Bear with each other and forgive one another if any of you has a grievance against someone. Forgive as the Lord forgave you.
(Colossians 3:13)

For if you forgive others when they sin against you, your heavenly Father will also forgive you. But if you do not forgive others their sins, your Father will not forgive your sins.
(Matthew 6:14–15)

There is no future without forgiveness.
(Archbishop Desmond Tutu)

CALLED TO FORGIVE

Practising surrender can be even more challenging when it includes forgiveness. The story of humanity is beset with damaging conversations, unscrupulous actions and relational breakdowns that run so deep it leaves little hope for reconciliation. Perhaps it seems strange, then, that Jesus would be so unequivocal about forgiveness. It's not something He merely suggests or describes as a nice thing to do. It's a clear, consistent command ringing through the Scriptures:

You have heard that it was said, 'Love your neighbour and hate your enemy.' But I tell you, love your enemies and pray for those who persecute you.'

And when you stand praying, if you hold anything against anyone, forgive them, so that your Father in heaven may forgive you your sins.[2]

Be merciful, just as your Father is merciful. Do not judge, and you will not be judged. Do not condemn, and you will not be condemned. Forgive, and you will be forgiven.[3]

Jesus doesn't just call Christians to a different pattern of behaviour; He calls for a radically different attitude in the human heart.

Many occasions when Jesus spoke of forgiveness are illustrated in the Greek New Testament by the use of the word *apheimi*. As a legal term, *apheimi* meant the cancellation of legal proceedings and the release from guilt and punishment. More broadly it meant to let go, to leave alone. Forgiveness means to let it go – let go of the words, the person, the wounds, the situation. The IOUs that lie on the floor of our decimated relationships are swept away. Nothing is owed us any more. Forgiveness means that it's over, it's finished.

WHEN IS ENOUGH?

But what if it is not finished? It's one thing to let go of the person driving recklessly on the journey to work, or the person who pushed in front of us at the supermarket. But how do we let go when it involves something that continues to happen – the lies told by a spouse, the unethical behaviour of a work colleague that costs us professionally for months to come? How do we forgive when we are reminded daily of how we were let down as we raise our family alone? What about when it seems we are taken for granted? Someone recognises they have failed us, they say they are sorry, but then they fail us again. How many times before we no longer need to forgive? Is there ever a limit? 'Even if they sin against you seven times in a day and seven times come back to you saying "I repent," you must forgive them.'[4]

Peter probably speaks for many of Jesus' disciples in Matthew 18 when he asks Jesus exactly how many times he is expected to forgive. Perhaps he has a particular person in mind, who knows? We often do. We can accept that forgiveness is required in some cases, but surely not with *that* person – the woman who cheated on you, the man who lied to you, the friend who stole from you.

Jesus replies 'seventy-seven times' (Matthew 18:22), which is a large number of offences to keep track of. Yet as the text notes in many of our Bibles indicate, some manuscripts of the Gospel record Jesus' reply as 'seventy times seven', which, if you're still counting, brings you to a limit of 490 times! After forgiving that person 490 times, are we finally in the clear?

Perhaps because Jesus knew Peter and every other one of His disciples so well, He tells a parable of an unmerciful servant to inject some much-needed perspective into our situation (Matthew 18:21–35). He speaks of a servant in huge debt to his master. The servant owed his master millions; it was a debt that could never be repaid. The only solution for repaying the debt was to sell the servant and his entire family into slavery. In hopeless desperation, the servant begs and pleads with the king for mercy. Miraculously, the king cancels the colossal debt and lets him go. As the servant walks free, he comes across a fellow servant who owes him ten pounds. The freed servant violently demands the money back. He ignores the indebted servant's pleas for mercy and has him imprisoned until the debt is paid. When the king hears of this, he confronts the first servant:

'You wicked servant,' he said, 'I cancelled all that debt of yours because you begged me to. Shouldn't you have had mercy on your fellow-servant, just as I had on you?'[5]

The king sends the servant to prison until he can pay off the original debt. In case the point of this story isn't clear, Jesus explains it:

> This is how my heavenly Father will treat each of you unless you forgive a brother or sister from your heart.[6]

The command to forgive is not insensitivity on Jesus' part. Forgiveness does not mean that what happened to us was excusable or acceptable. The call to forgiveness does not ignore your feelings and experiences. The call to forgiveness is *in view of God's mercy*. We've messed up too. We have wounded and crushed people with our words and actions. We have thought, said and done things that were simply wrong. Despite our best behaviour, our wrongdoing leaves a debt we cannot pay. And in the face of a crushing debt that would enslave us for ever, Jesus stepped in and died for us.

> You see, at just the right time, when we were still powerless, Christ died for the ungodly. Very rarely will anyone die for a righteous person, though for a good person someone might possibly dare to die. But God demonstrates his own love for us in this: while we were still sinners, Christ died for us.
>
> Since we have now been justified by his blood, how much more shall we be saved from God's wrath through him! For if, while we were God's enemies, we were reconciled to him through the death of his Son, how much more, having been reconciled, shall we be saved through his life![7]

THE IMPOSSIBLE MADE POSSIBLE

When we look at another person's wrongdoings we can justify our reasons to withhold forgiveness. But when we remember Jesus, it's far more difficult to explain it away. Still, it's not easy. Some of us are wrestling with unspeakable offences committed against us or those we love. Even in view of His mercy, forgiveness seems impossible, even if we wanted to offer it. In her book *The Hiding Place*, Corrie ten Boom speaks of forgiveness in the midst of horrendous circumstances. She tells the story of her family in the Netherlands, who sheltered Jews during the Nazi occupation. When an informant infiltrated their home, the Ten Booms were arrested and imprisoned. Corrie and her sister Betsie were sent to Ravensbrück, a women's concentration camp. Throughout her time there Betsie extended love and forgiveness to all, even the Nazis who treated her cruelly. Betsie later died in the camp.

After the war, Corrie travelled the world with a message of love and forgiveness. But her message was tested on a personal level at a service in Munich. Corrie was approached by one of the former SS guards from Ravensbrück, now a committed Christian. The SS guards were responsible for unspeakable brutality: how was she to love one of the men responsible for the torture she and Betsie suffered, and for Betsie's death? As the man reached out to shake her hand, Corrie was flooded with anger and 'vengeful thoughts'. She prayed for God to enable her to do what she couldn't, and He gave her the strength to shake that man's hand:

> And so I discovered that it is not on our forgiveness any more than on our goodness that the world's healing hinges, but on His. When He tells us to love our enemies, He gives, along with the command, the love itself.[8]

Can God make an impossible act of forgiveness possible? As we think of forgiveness in view of God's mercy, we are reminded that on the cross God took on the pain and injustice we suffered, so that we would experience His life and wholeness. The prophet Isaiah writes the following in a prophecy ultimately fulfilled in Jesus:

Surely he took up our pain
and bore our suffering,
yet we considered him punished by God,
stricken by him, and afflicted.
But he was pierced for our transgressions,
he was crushed for our iniquities;
the punishment that brought us peace was on him,
and by his wounds we are healed.[9]

Will the cross be the place we go for forgiveness for the sins we have committed, *and* for healing from the sins committed against us? Will we approach Him with the bitter pain of adultery, the anger of betrayal, the wounds left by rejection? Or will we choose to hold on to unforgiveness and in doing so reject the healing that Christ can bring?

THE POWER OF UNFORGIVENESS

It's not surprising that in Matthew 18, Jesus calls us to forgive from our hearts, the epicentre of our lives. Unforgiveness can wield incredible power. Sometimes we can believe that a refusal to forgive somehow gives us control and indicates our strength in a tough situation. We are mistaken. Unforgiveness can actually hold us captive. Jesus is clear that unforgiveness has a powerful impact on the quality of our relationship with God:

For if you forgive others when they sin against you, your heavenly Father will also forgive you. But if you do not forgive others their sins, your Father will not forgive your sins.[10]

When we hold on to unforgiveness, we struggle to access His mercy, grace and power in daily living. Unforgiveness consumes our thoughts and energies and leads to bitterness. Imagine that a confidence is betrayed at church by someone you thought was a good friend. The friendship is ruined, and there is no way forward. If we don't let it go from our hearts, we will find that unforgiveness will begin to affect our outlook on how we approach relationships in general. We trusted that person and they let us down badly; we won't trust anyone like that again; it's safer that way. The distances we create from others pollute our relationships, threatening their potential before they even begin. We may think we're stronger this way and have moved on, but in truth the damage that situation created is stronger than ever. It's no longer confined to the past. The past is present and shaping how we do life. As Archbishop Desmond Tutu says, 'There is no future without forgiveness.' Without forgiveness, all we have is living our lives in the shadows of the past, with things left unresolved.

There are occasions when unforgiveness can even affect our physical health (though it's worth stressing that not every sickness is the result of unforgiveness). I once had the opportunity to pray for a woman with arthritis. As we talked, she told me of a very painful divorce, saying, 'I know that my arthritis has something to do with this.' She had sought to forgive her ex-husband, but the ongoing difficulties devoured her heart again, ultimately having an impact on her physical well-being. When the time came to pray, the woman poured out her heart to God, as she let her ex-husband go again for what must have felt like the hundredth time. When I saw her a few days later, she noted that her body was being healed. At the end of the week, by the amazing grace of God, a transformation had taken place, inside and out.

When we surrender our hearts to God to help us forgive, we're transformed. Sometimes that transformation is swift. In other cases, it can be a long journey.

A JOURNEY OF FORGIVENESS

My father had not been involved in my life; I felt I'd been defined by his absence. I met him when I was twelve. It was such a strange feeling to be so angry at someone and yet so desperately longing for his love, approval and comfort. I felt that way for many years as birthdays and Christmases came and went, knowing he was not there and was probably never going to be. I'd hoped that in my twenties it would be easier, that I would need him less. But when my roommates' dads would come and take us all out for dinner one night, or help fix the house, or send their kids a little bit of extra cash, I felt the loss all over again. I did still need him, but he still wasn't there. It culminated on the day I bought a new car. I felt this strange restlessness all day. That night I walked the streets in tears, waiting for my pain to find words. Finally I blurted out, 'It was meant to be your day! You were supposed to be here and you weren't. Again!' I'd had enough. I'd forgiven so many times and nothing had changed. I was beyond disappointed; tired of feeling angry. Now I just felt cold.

A few months later, I attended a conference and stumbled on a seminar about forgiveness. If I'd known what it was about, I might have avoided it! The woman who led this seminar gave a gentle yet clear challenge about forgiveness. She described it as tearing up the IOUs, explaining that if we had fully forgiven someone, they didn't owe us anything any more. They were completely free and, ultimately, so were we. I was so angry at her.

At the end of the session, as people received prayer or sat reading their Bibles, I was in a corner, crying hard, arguing with – well, more like *at* – God. I held on to many grievances, some petty, some self-righteous, some painful. There was some heartbreak here and there. Gossipy words from school, racial abuse in the street – not the easiest things to let go of. But all these paled into insignificance when compared to my attitude to my father. It was not the first time I'd faced this. There had been many tears, and a lot of healing over the years. But this was a step too far for me.

'Lord, how can you say he owes me nothing?' I sobbed. 'He owes me everything, he owes me a father. Birthdays, and Christmas! He owes me hugs and love, teenage arguments and slammed doors. He owes me my childhood! And now you want me to let that go, to say it's not important, that I am not important? What am I to you?'

In moments like that I find the truth hard to hear, but also essential. The truth was that I was important to God – so important that he sent His Son so that I could be free from life's wounds, but also free from my own sin. Kneeling there, sobbing, holding my Bible, I knew. I knew I needed to let go. I just didn't want to. Not yet.

My mind filled with memories of my wounds, but also my many mistakes. I'm no innocent. There were words I'd said, things I'd done, wounds I'd inflicted. How could I have been so cruel and heartless, so self-centred that I didn't even care how my actions would affect others? I cried over those too. In the same prayer I was saying how sorry I was and how justified I was to stay bitter. I knew I had to move forward somehow. All I could do at that moment was to say that I was willing to go on the journey if God could get me there. I wasn't even sure what letting go looked like.

When I got home, I knew it was time to write a letter to my dad. It was not one of my usual stiff, awkward ones, but an honest, open one. I wrote to Dad and told him of the conference and the healing I was receiving. Then I told him that if he didn't want to write any more, he was free to stop and that was fine, I wouldn't hold it over him. I said I was sorry for my attitude, and for my less-than-pleasant letters sent over the years. Then I said that if he did want to start again, I'd like to see what kind of relationship we could build. I posted the letter, and then I waited.

And waited. And waited. After it seemed certain that the Nigerian mailing system had finished the work of developing patience in my character, a letter finally arrived from my dad. I wasn't sure we were off to the most promising start when I saw it was labelled 'To Joan'. (No disrespect to anyone called Joan, but it's not my name and when the letter is from your estranged dad in the middle of a reconciliation, getting the name wrong makes you feel a bit tense!)

The letter was . . . great. He said he was pleased with my letter, saying that if that was what God could do, then perhaps God could work in his life too. He asked me to pray for him, and yes, to keep writing. It didn't change the past. We were still strangers. But slowly we began to build our own quirky father-daughter thing. Our letters were as sporadic as ever, but now we included the occasional phone call. Something good was emerging from the wreckage of our story, and I liked it.

About a year ago, my sister got in touch saying Dad had asked me to call. It was odd: he'd never asked us to get in touch. I was going to leave it for another day, but suddenly changed my mind and called.

'Jo, is that you?'

'Yes, Dad.' He started crying hard, sobbing and wailing. 'What's wrong?'

'I don't know.'

Between the crackly phone line and my dad's loud sobbing, it was hard to understand him. He'd been in hospital and was having tests. And he kept thanking me, telling me he was glad I called.

For some reason I'll never know, I said, 'Dad, you need to understand that I'm OK. And that you and I are OK. The past was over a long time ago. I'm OK, I'm doing well. And you and me, we're OK now. Do you know that, Dad?'

He responded in agreement. It's amazing how the phrase 'OK' can say so much.

I continued. 'But you're not at peace, and God wants that with you and you need to make peace with Him.' So we prayed on the phone. He cried even harder.

Soon, way too soon, it was time to go. He was calmer now. I said I'd call again. He thanked me again and said goodbye.

'Goodbye. I love you, Dad.'

He died about two weeks later.

I was thirty-four when my father died, and my journey of forgiveness and healing spanned many years. There was a lot to deal with, a lot of confusion and hurt. There were good days when I was filled with love and freedom, and bad days when I was entrenched in anger and bitterness. But God carried me through. He didn't indulge me; the words from Scripture on forgiveness were not adapted for my situation, and sometimes that was very hard to take. So I gave Him my will – saying I *chose* to forgive, though the feelings weren't there. I gave Him my thoughts, filled with reasons why this was a bad idea! I gave Him my sadness and pain. They were feelings that had echoed through my childhood and were still there shaping my womanhood. I learned to give Him my heart, and it was a struggle at times. But I received forgiveness, healing and freedom to walk into the future.

Sometimes forgiveness is a journey, and like all those great journeys in life, it begins with the first step.

Q. Are you ready to take the first step in practising forgiveness?

FIRST STEPS IN FORGIVENESS

The first step in practising forgiveness will be different for each one of us, simply because the situations in life are so different. Letting go of an insensitive comment someone made is different from letting go of the lies and gossip in the office that have affected your career. Forgiveness for the person who scratched your car is different from forgiving an unfaithful spouse or a sexual assault. Sometimes our struggle with unforgiveness is deeply connected to wounds we have received through life. There may be events in our history that had a huge impact on us and are not fully resolved. It will be vital that we talk to someone – a family member or close friend, a church leader, a qualified counsellor. In specific situations we may need to consider contacting the police. There are unique situations which need to be handled in a specific way, and God accompanies us on that journey. Then there are the everyday offences that we encounter: a harsh word here, an inconsiderate action there. We find ourselves in a situation where a particular person is getting on our nerves. We've reached the end of our tether. What do we do?

IDEAS FOR PRACTISING FORGIVENESS

Again, I don't think there's a mathematical equation for these things, but some things can help us practise forgiveness. There are practices that we can adopt that attend to every area of our hearts (will, thoughts, emotions, etc.). Sometimes *we need to admit something is wrong*. A friend of mine once said, 'I used to think that I was the most forgiving person around. Then I realised that I was just the most bitter.' It may sound like a counterintuitive comment, but sometimes we dismiss our frustrations too quickly. We'd rather dismiss our feelings than confront a person. So we pretend that we've thought it through and let it go, but somehow the issues remain. We become overcritical of that person; we might even resent them. We find it easier to talk about them, put them down a little (or a lot). When someone else talks about them negatively, we agree and secretly feel justified in our opinions. Alternatively, we say we've let something go, but slammed doors, heaving sighs and clipped answers of 'I'm fine' suggest otherwise! The frustration is still there; we're just in passive-aggressive mode.

Another thing to consider when practising forgiveness is *our expectations*. Did that person do something wrong, or did they do something you didn't expect? Was that job really yours, or was the interviewer entitled to give it to someone else? You thought that girl was going to be your wife, but was she wrong to end the relationship when she realised she was not committed to you? It can be hard to distinguish between unfulfilled expectations and actual wrongdoing at times, especially when pain is involved. Sometimes we hurt because life can be painful, not because someone intended to wound us. Did that person mean to hurt us, or was it one of those no-win situations?

A great place to begin to admit that something is wrong and to consider our expectations is in prayer. We can share our disappointments, our negative thoughts, our angry words. We can pray about the situation, but also pray for the person involved as the Bible instructs.[11] This may be the last thing you feel like doing, but really, who could be better to talk to than God? Who else is going to enable you to forgive from your heart? Prayer might not come easily at first; your prayers might start with lots of self-justifying opinions, or with expressions of pain. But it's a wonderful chance for God to get to work on our hearts.

Still, not all we do in this area can be internal. In Matthew 18, prior to the parable of the unmerciful servant, Jesus offers a practical solution for times when someone has offended us: *talk to the person involved*!

> If a brother or sister sins, go and point out the fault, just between the two of you. If they listen to you, you have won them over. But if they will not listen, take one or two others along, so that 'every matter may be established by the testimony of two or three witnesses.' If they still refuse to listen, tell it to

the church; and if they refuse to listen even to the church, treat them as you would a pagan or a tax collector.[12]

How many times have we observed this process in reverse? A conflict occurs and word gets spread across a church community first. People take sides, individuals feel judged. The conflict is dissected in twos or threes, interpreting and reinterpreting who said/did/felt what. It's an all-too-tantalising opportunity to air our grievances and get the last word in gossipy conversations. By the time the people actually involved face one another, there's more than just the original conflict to deal with. How many of our everyday conflicts would be diffused or resolved, if we simply took the first step Jesus suggested of directly addressing the person involved with a view to working things out?

Could you arrange to meet for coffee, away from likely interruptions, and try to work it out alone?

Practising forgiveness is hard work, but it has a transforming effect on our relationships. We'll find we have good days, bad days, petty days, sad days. What matters is that in view of God's mercy, we draw on His resources to choose to forgive, to be willing to choose to forgive, to be willing to be willing. Don't allow this process with the Lord to stagnate, but if you do – reach out to God and start again. Unforgiveness can be like a toxin that pollutes the life in our relationship with God. *Choose forgiveness.*

5
How to practise in pain

You've kept track of my every toss and turn
through the sleepless nights,
Each tear entered in your ledger,
each ache written in your book.
(Psalm 56:8 *The Message*)

The Lord is close to the broken-hearted
and saves those who are crushed in spirit.
(Psalm 34:18 NIV)

Life is difficult.
(M. Scott Peck, *The Road Less Travelled*)

AN ANATOMY LESSON

In a classic *Grey's Anatomy* episode (I've probably alienated half of
you right there, but try to stay with me), Dr Meredith Grey visits
her mum Ellis in her private hospital room. Ellis Grey, once a
legendary surgeon, is now in an advanced stage of Alzheimer's. By
some strange made-for-TV-drama miracle, she has one day of
lucidity, the first in five years. Inevitably she wants to spend time
with Meredith. Their relationship has never been easy, and this
meeting is no exception. Ellis disapproves of Meredith's life choices
and relationships, accusing her of being unfocused and ordinary.

'I raised you to be extraordinary – what happened to you?'

Later, in another painful exchange, Meredith finally garners the
courage to respond to the woman who has overshadowed her life.

'You want to know why I'm so unfocused, so ordinary? You want to know what happened to me? YOU. *You happened to me!*'

BROKEN LIVES, BROKEN HEARTS

We expected that life would be extraordinary. Then life happened to us. As M. Scott Peck said, 'Life is difficult.' People happened to us and, as we saw in the last chapter, people can be difficult too, relationships can be hard and painful. Furthermore, though Jesus promised 'life to the full' in John 10:10, we sometimes forget that in the preceding verse He speaks of an enemy, the devil who seeks to steal, kill and destroy our lives. The spiritual battles we endure in life can overwhelm us at times. Unlike on TV, the episodes of life don't resolve easily and neatly on the hour. We go through events, experiences and relationships that shape, define and damage us. Our hearts – thoughts, will, desires, affections, dreams – are changed for ever when life happens. While I thanked God for saving my baby's life, others wept over a miscarriage or infertility. While some celebrate a new job and financial provision, others wonder through sleepless nights how they'll keep their home, now that their job has gone. While some families experience miraculous reconciliation, still others fall apart. Some sing of God's freedom and deliverance, while others hide, ashamed of the secret struggles and behaviour patterns that contradict what they publicly believe. Some have been ill for years now, and yes, they've prayed for healing. Some cannot move into the future because they are paralysed by the past. We face situations in everyday life that have no easy answers or no answer at all. Or we live with news or a diagnosis that casts a shadow over our future. Life is hard on the heart sometimes. Some days we're barely making it through.

Where is God when our hearts are broken? Where is His love

in the brutality of our own personal nightmares? Can we still walk with Him, when we look at our lives and question His goodness and His greatness?

Sometimes, if we're honest, we just fake it to get by. We're funny types, we Christians. We can talk and sing of blessing and victory, while inside we're emotionally bankrupt and feel defeated. We'll wear our masks at church/work/home by day and cry alone at night. A mask seems easier than wrestling with our crisis and our God. So we push it aside and get on with the real business of praying hard, reading our Bibles and being Good Christian People. Maybe it works for a while. But underneath our hearts are still bleeding and that will ultimately affect our relationship with God, whether we acknowledge it or not. As Proverbs says, 'Hope deferred makes the heart sick.'[1] When life doesn't happen the way we hoped, the way we'd expected it to be, we get heartsick. When we're heartsick, our perception of God's goodness and greatness changes. Uncertain of who He is, we find it harder to surrender, to forgive, to be thankful. Unsettled by what we've experienced, we question how much we can trust Him. Even when we want to, sometimes we find we're just not able. It's hard to be close to God, to grow with Him. Sometimes heartsickness takes us from the centre of Christian community and casts us into its sidelines and shadows. In some cases we walk away from our relationship with God completely.

HOW TO PRACTISE IN PAIN

In an ideal made-for-TV world, we'd be able to resolve all of life's tough situations almost painlessly. We'd find the perfect formula for our relationship with God. Heartsickness would heal neatly and privately. Unfortunately, real life is not made for TV and a person's heartsickness is a unique experience. 'Each heart knows its own bitterness,'[2] notes the writer of Proverbs, and it refuses to be neatly packaged. It doesn't look as neat and tidy as other seasons of our life. Heartsickness is raw and messy, stained with tears. It's punctuated with outbursts of frustration, or numbed silence, sometimes all in the same day. Rather than pretend and mask our struggles and heartsickness, what could it look like to walk with God through them instead?

The Bible often captures the stories of human heartache. In its pages we read of family conflicts, marital struggles and breakdown, infertility, slavery and oppression, sickness, pain and loss. Bad things happen to both bad and good people. The songs and prayers of the Bible articulate the cries of people's hearts responding to God in difficult times. Sometimes we find declarations of confidence in the face of difficulty.

When I am afraid, I put my trust in you.[3]

Sometimes we find songs and prayers of lament and despair.

My heart is in anguish within me;
the terrors of death have fallen on me.
Fear and trembling have beset me;
horror has overwhelmed me.[4]

So how do we learn to do this today? We've often misinterpreted our relationship with God, assuming that we need to have it all together even when it's all falling apart. It can be hard even to admit in these times that our faith has taken something of a battering. We end up repressing everything or denying it – neither of which is helpful. Is there a way to do this? This chapter doesn't exist to come up with an easy six-point formula, wonderful though it would be! What we have instead are stories of people who have journeyed with God through some of life's darkest valleys, and the lessons and experiences they had along the way. Through their stories, their testimonies, we'll find something that perhaps can help us say in our hearts:

Put your hope in God,
for I will yet praise him,
my Saviour and my God.[5]

'TRUST WAS SHATTERED ON EVERY LEVEL'

The Israelites were enslaved for 430 years before Moses led them to freedom in the exodus. But even though they were physically free, it became evident that in many ways they were still enslaved. They were unable to entrust their lives to God. In times of crisis they would even cry out for their old life in Egypt (Exodus 16:3; 17:3).

Though few of us have known physical slavery, some of us have been enslaved by events in our lives. It could be sexual abuse or physical violence, or abuse of a mental and emotional kind. It could be a horrendous accident or event that devastated your family. Whatever it was, it defined your life and tore through your heart. Can God reach us there? Here's Megan's story.

Like many Christian teenage girls, Megan was trying to work out how to be a godly girl and be pure in her relationships with boys. She went to her youth leader for wisdom and advice. But Megan's trust was shattered on every level when her youth leader, married with a family, took advantage of her. She had no way to deal with what had happened. A few years later, a lifelong family friend and respected figure in her church and community made an inappropriate advance towards her. Megan felt trapped and confused, again with no one to talk to. She drove away into the night in tears, feeling utterly alone. The events defined her relationships with men for years to come.

Years later, in a new country and a different life, it was time to address Megan's life-defining moments:

> He had to tackle the evening; I drove into the night. I was brought back to loneliness, that disbelief. I felt like God said to me, 'That evening, I wept with you.'
>
> I so needed to hear that; that God was for me, that He was with me.
>
> But I also needed to hear that He didn't want me to stay in the broken place I was in.
>
> I realised I could wrestle with questions, but at the end of the day I may never get answers. The big question I needed to answer was, 'Do I want a relationship with God, or decide never to talk to Him again?'
>
> Isaiah 62:11 says: 'Say to the Daughter of Zion, See, your Saviour comes! . . . and you will be called Sought After, the City No Longer Deserted.' His Word was healing. Slowly over time I learned to choose to hold onto God's Word. It was difficult at times. I realised that the enemy uses these events to hold us captive. We can't move forward, trapped in our anger at God and our pain. But I discovered as I kept on walking with Him, even when it was hard, my chains fell off and I found freedom.

Megan was trapped and defined by the circumstances of her past, until God's Word broke in with life and freedom. Megan's story reminds us that God's Word is not just relevant; it is living and active, as Hebrews 4:12 says, working powerfully in our lives, leading us into truth and freedom.

Q. How does the Bible speak to you when you're going through tough times? What do you think God might be saying to you through the circumstances of your life right now?

'WHAT DID I DO TO DESERVE THIS?'

I went away full, but the LORD has brought me back empty . . .
The LORD has afflicted me; the Almighty has brought misfortune
upon me.[6]

These were Naomi's words, reflecting on her years in Moab where she lost her husband and both her sons. Her loss was so devastating that she told her community they should no longer call her Naomi, which meant 'pleasant', but Mara, meaning 'bitter'. When our lives are ripped apart by tragedy and grief, sometimes a relationship with God seems impossible. Becky shares her journey through her darkest hours:

30 December 2006 is a day which changed my life for ever and
the consequences of which meant that nothing in my life will
ever be the same again. My beautiful husband of eighteen
months, John, died aged twenty-eight, of illness, with no
warning. I was six months pregnant at the time. Not only did I
lose my best friend, my lover, my companion and my favourite
person, but I also lost the father of my child, my hopes and
dreams for the future, I lost my home, I lost the belief and hope
that life is fundamentally good and safe. The very grounds of all
that I had believed and based my life upon had been shaken to
the core. The time that has passed since that day has been full
of indescribable pain, total and overwhelming love, loneliness,
hope, despair, confusion, unbelievable anger and questioning
things to distraction!
    What I have known above all else, even in the midst of my

biggest tantrums towards God, is that His everlasting arms are holding me. It has been a difficult journey back to trusting God again and at times I feared I would never get back there. There are still moments when I scream, 'Why have you let this happen to my lovely family? What did I do to deserve this? Are you trustworthy for my future?'

Dare you ask God the difficult questions? Dare you confront the depths of pain in your heart that affect your relationship with God?

The Psalms have room for such raw honesty: Psalm 22 begins, 'My God, my God, why have you forsaken me?'[7] – words that Jesus himself cried out on the cross. God wants access to the pain, even the anger towards Him that lurks behind our masks. He's not just committed in the good times of our relationship. He was redeeming Naomi's life, even when she blamed Him for her situation.

Becky's journey continues to move from tragedy to healing:

But now (two years and nearly four months on) I can sit here and say that I am a truly blessed woman – I knew the love of an amazing man who gave me so much. Although the time we spent together was so short in terms of my potential life span the impact he had on my life will always be immense. I have been given the most beautiful daughter. I have known the love of friends, family and strangers to a point where I am often reduced to tears. I have been blessed with deepened friendships, healed friendships, new friendships, which even in my anger towards God reminded me deep down that God does provide and does restore. I have known material provision. I have known protection emotionally. The prayers, the words, the gifts, the experiences and the people that have blessed me could in themselves fill a book. I may never know this side of heaven why John was taken from me, but I have to choose to believe that through God life can be good again, I can love again, I can have more children, I can know deep joy again, that God can heal the hurt and pain and bring good from it all, but it is not easy to do that. It is a choice I have to make every day, but I need to choose it because I know that I want a better life for me and my little girl and not a life of bitterness. I know, as it's been proved time and time again in my life over the last few years, I cannot do that without Him.

'THE BOTTOM DROPPED OUT OF OUR WORLD'

Doug and Angela were on the cusp of a new phase of life filled with opportunities. Doug was completing his MBA, Angela was pregnant with their second child who would join two-year-old Theo and complete their family. They lived in Phoenix, Arizona, but knew they would relocate soon; the destination ultimately depended on Doug's new job. Angela felt a combination of stress and excitement for what lay ahead. Doug felt the pressure in a different way. He embraced the adventure, but he wanted to provide for his family. 'I gave everything to it, pushing all the doors. I put in 100 per cent prayer and 100 per cent action. I applied for 200 jobs, and went for 75 interviews.' But something was about to happen that would change everything.

Doug had been having problems with his sight in his left eye, and had undergone an MRI scan before Christmas. The scan found a benign tumour in the cavity where the optic nerve meets the brain. Initially they expected that he would need some minor laser treatment. However, the neurosurgeon told Doug that the tumour needed to be removed. The only way to do it was through a craniotomy, an incredibly invasive operation. And the eyesight Doug had lost in his left eye would not be restored. The operation would take place in three weeks – one week before the new baby was due.

Doug and Angela were reeling. 'I was in shock,' said Angela. 'I couldn't think straight to organise anything. We were literally and figuratively in the desert: no friends, family or community. Normally Doug and I are reasonably confident and capable, in control of life. Now, suddenly, life had veered totally out of control. We felt utterly hopeless and unable to cope. I prayed the only words I could utter at that point. "Lord, please meet our needs as I know they are great but I don't know what they are."'

'The bottom dropped out of our world,' said Doug. 'For me the breaking point came when I was walking in the desert listening to Brian Doerksen's version of Psalm 13. When I heard the words "But I trust in your unfailing love"[8] I broke down in tears under the pressure of it all. I had always been in control. Now I had no money, no job, and I couldn't be there when my baby was born. I had no choice but to hand it all over, the operation, our family, our future. Everything was surrendered to God, totally abandoned to God's will.'

The weeks that followed were filled with tears and fears, prayers and miracles. They found their every need provided for. Childcare, finances, meals were taken care of as people gathered around them. 'We were aware that blessings from heaven were pouring out all around us,' said Angela. 'And the Lord showed us a community we had no idea was there. Soon I could feel people's prayers as I was supernaturally calm. The Lord changed my heart and my prayers turned to incessant thankfulness that He was in control. Through many teary days I found myself repeating, "God is good. All the time."' Doug and Angela also began listening to and singing songs of worship and praise and triumph.

'We received so much prayer throughout that time,' said Doug.

'I went to church and a group gathered around me and prayed with me. On the morning of the operation a pastor drove two hours to be with us and pray.'

When they learned that morning that the tumour had grown, the reality hit them hard. The operation took seven hours, much longer than expected. Still, the neurosurgeon was pleased; the operation was incredibly successful. The recovery had begun.

Angela returned to the hospital the following day and curled up on the bed with Doug as he dozed in and out from the effects of the morphine. Grateful, exhausted and overwhelmed, she kept trying to pray, but couldn't find the words. It didn't matter. 'Before I could say anything else, I saw Jesus sitting there in the room with us, plain as day. He said, "Can't you see me? I'm right here." It's like He was gently saying, "Angela, is it not obvious to you yet? Just relax and know that I am here with you."'

Doug was released a week later. He could barely walk and couldn't see. Noise and movement hurt him; all he could do was lie in bed. With fifty staples on his head, eight metal plates and fourteen screws holding his skull back in place, he was unrecognisable. He could listen to music, though, so songs of worship and praise continued to fill their home. Doug recovered well. Contrary to expectations, Doug's sight was fully restored. Their baby, a daughter, was a week late, giving Doug more recovery time! They described her as 'our precious gift after the storm'. Then one of the companies Doug had been interviewed by in December called to see if he was still available.

Four years (and two more beautiful children!) later, Doug and Angela reflected upon their journey. Doug said: 'Our experience brought me closer to God. I'm more of a man in God now, my strength is in Him, I depend on Him; He's my first port of call.' Angela echoed similar sentiments on a closer relationship with the Lord, adding, 'Today I have a quiet confidence in the fact that no matter what is going on, God will supply all our needs.' And they both continually testify to the power of God, and the power of prayer.

Like each of these stories, there are so many encouragements, so many things we can learn. But I am struck most by Doug and Angela's testimony regarding prayer and worship. It would have been the last thing they felt like doing; but they met God in such a powerful way. Can we find ways to reach out for God in the worst of times, knowing that He is still God and Good? And when we can't – will we allow people to pray with us, encourage us? Will we pray and worship and fight with others in their struggle?

'JESUS, THE MAN OF MANY SORROWS, IS HERE'

Some of our struggles don't concern a one-off event, but an ongoing situation we're dealing with in life. This is Dan's story.

In early 2003 I was diagnosed with multiple sclerosis. I didn't know much about it then other than that it was probably a Bad Thing, but we'd started to have a lot of teaching on physical healing at our church so I thought it would only be a prayer meeting or two until I got healed. I only had a couple of mild symptoms at the time and I certainly didn't think the illness would progress that much – that would be a Really Bad Thing. I'd spent my whole life thinking that Really Bad Things only ever happen to Other People; God would never let me get very ill, or so I thought. But my health deteriorated, new symptoms came along (numbness, weakness, fatigue, pain, spasms, incontinence, cognitive problems, tinnitus, to name a few) and I now use a wheelchair, so I've had to question what I thought I believed. We've probably all heard talks about Moses' forty years in the desert or Joseph being sold into slavery and wrongly imprisoned before they could be used by God and fulfil their purpose. I would tell myself that they went through those kinds of experiences so I wouldn't have to. They had to experience the desert in order to learn to die to self and depend on God; now we can learn those lessons just by hearing a sermon and knowing in our head what the theory and process is. However, I've found that head knowledge rarely transforms the heart as much as actual experience.

When I was at my absolute lowest with the MS – effectively paralysed from the waist down, subject to overwhelming fatigue, in pain and, worst of all, feeling abandoned by God, people would say to me God knew how I felt. I know they meant well, but it didn't help me. If anything, it made me angrier with God. I wanted to give up on Him, because I thought He'd given up on me and let me down. This wasn't what I'd been led to expect from God, this caring Father who could perform miracles and overcome any problem with ease. Surely God wants us living in the Promised Land right now, where we're fully healed and living in abundant fruitfulness. It was our God-given right, and any kind of wilderness experience should be prayed against. The fact that this wasn't my reality was why I wanted to give up on God. The reason I didn't was the voice I kept getting in my head, saying simply, 'Now you know how I felt.' I had no answer to that.

The Promised Land may be where we're heading, but the fact is we're not all there yet. While it may be promised, simply saying we 'should' be there is not enough. How do we live in the 'not yet'? How do we respond to those who are living in the 'not yet'? Being told God wants me well hasn't had much lasting effect on my faith. What has helped me more is being able to find God in the right now, regardless of my circumstance.

I certainly wouldn't be choosing to engage with this desert journey of dying to self if I wasn't ill. Why would I? I know in my head that my identity is as a child of God, but I'd get more worth and security than I'd care to admit from my ministry or appearance or job or possessions or abilities. I still do, but I'm slowly starting to see that maybe I can be free of these things, things that are going to pass away anyway. Paul getting his identity and security from God was probably part of his learning the secret of being content, regardless of how much he had.

I've heard disabled people say they're not disabled; it's society that disables them. How can we serve and enable those in a state of dis-ease? Do we eagerly pray for people in hardship at first, only to drift away when nothing changes? Or do we process with them, with God and in ourselves all the possible stages of grief and the feelings that come up, and the challenges to our faith? Not giving glib answers, not solving the problem. Just sitting with people in their pain, allowing them to share the gift of their lives and experiences, finding God in the silence. Because when two people are gathered in His name, Jesus, that man of many sorrows, is there.

So I'm still living in the 'not yet'. I'd love to say I've travelled through my desert and everything's lovely now. But the fact is, I have an incurable, degenerative disease. I'm only thirty-two and already a wheelchair-user. My prognosis is not cheery. I may get physically healed one day, but it's not happened yet. So I don't have much choice but to treat the MS as my thorn in the flesh, reminding me to lose my life, to surrender to my desert, to let it strip me of my false identity, to take up my cross daily and learn to lean on my lover. Sometimes that feels like death; sometimes I'm thankful for the process. I'm slowly getting better at seeing where God already is in my life, even when all I can do is lie in bed exhausted. It's like when you turn the lights out at night; at first it seems pitch black, but slowly your eyes become adjusted and you start to discover that you can see things because there's more light than you realised. It means I'm not quite so afraid of the dark, knowing that God's in the night with me. While I'm waiting for the dawn I want to make it my aim to have my identity so much in God that I don't need to be healed. If I can do that, then I'll probably already be in the Promised Land.

Isaiah states prophetically of Jesus that:

He was despised and rejected by others,
a man of suffering, and familiar with pain.[9]

Yet it's not the picture of Jesus that we tend to be most comfortable with. Perhaps the Jesus we prefer to reflect on and sing to is more victorious and triumphant. It's the truth, Jesus has conquered sin and death and hell, and it is wonderful to declare it. Still, it's important to know the full picture. Jesus was rejected throughout His ministry, getting abuse and death threats. He was betrayed by a close friend. He was tortured and abused, and mocked throughout. He was crucified like a violent criminal. And He was completely innocent. Jesus the victor understands suffering and pain. He understands our suffering and pain. Rather than being completely alienated, Dan was reminded that he journeyed with a God who not only loved him, but intimately understood pain and suffering.

'MY BLUES TURNED TO GREY'

Finally there are times when we are simply unable to connect with God. Life is so overwhelming that there are no prayers to pray and God doesn't seem to be speaking. And yet . . .

When Zoë was born, I couldn't wait to leave the hospital. After Tia's birth, I'd been chained to an IV due to pre-eclampsia and had to be closely monitored. This time I felt euphoric, healthy and fit. I was eager to go home and get on with life. Home in twenty-four hours, I blogged about my experiences before I even went to bed. Zoë, my sweet victory, was finally here in my arms.

After the euphoria came the baby blues as my body adjusted, but I was ready for that. I just wasn't ready for what came next. The baby blues turned to grey.

It was as though heavy, dark grey clouds unfolded and surrounded me, threatening to consume me. I couldn't give my newborn a bath: I was terrified I'd hurt her. I couldn't take the girls out of the house, just in case I did something wrong. My world was getting smaller and darker as everyday functional tasks became insurmountable. Initially I tried to put it down to sleepless nights and an exponential increase in the laundry – until I went to a coffee shop and drove away in tears because I couldn't decide what to order. Then I went to a friend's house and I couldn't get out of the car because I was so paralysed by fear. I actually had to pray to take each step towards the door. Ten feet took ten minutes. Driving home, I felt helpless and hopeless, my life utterly worthless. What was the point in even being here? What good was I to these precious children? I might as well . . .

I didn't realise my husband had been watching me closely. He'd noticed that I was becoming distant and fearful. He sat and listened as I began. 'I don't know what's wrong with me, but something is wrong . . .' When I finished he retrieved a leaflet from our bedroom, which he'd felt prompted to pick up months ago when visiting a hospital. It was all about post-natal depression and it might as well have had my name on it. I went to the doctor's the following day. My doctor listened, asked questions, and recommended three things: anti-depressants, regular exercise and counselling.

Time stood still. Chronologically, the days continued, of course. Some of them were very dark, some of them were OK, and some had glimpses of light and hope. But none of them would tell me what tomorrow would be like or when it would end.

And what about my relationship with God? I needed Him more than I needed air. But I couldn't pray, or read my Bible. I found church really difficult; there were too many people. My mind was either overloaded with thoughts or completely drained. I was numb. But there was a song on repeat in my car for at least a month. It was 29th Chapter's remix of Tim Hughes's song 'When the Tears Fall'. Sometimes tears rolled as I drove; sometimes I was cold as stone. But the song continued to play. Thankfully, no one asked me to change the song.

I know late into the night when the tears fall, you hold me . . . when hope is lost, I'll call you Saviour . . .[10]

By The 29th Chapter/Tim Hughes
Copyright ©2006 & 2003 Thankyou Music.

God was there. Our relationship looked very different, but He was there. He was there in the kindness of a wonderful husband. He was there in a gentle doctor who checked up on me weekly. He was there with a prescription that acted like a cast on a limb while He tended to a broken life. He was there in the counselling (which reminded me of physiotherapy – a painful exercise that ultimately makes you stronger and whole, but was very stretching at the time). He was there in friends who asked how I was, and in friends who didn't ask, but just hung out with me, bought me Starbucks coffee and made me feel normal. He was there, ministering to me through my sweet little girls. I didn't feel the sense of a greater purpose in what I was going through. I didn't hear a still small voice in the storm. But through the people around me, every moment of the day, He held my hand.

Some days our journey with God may feel at a standstill, or worse, we may feel that we walk alone. Only hindsight reveals the journey we've made. The truth is that though God may not be visible, it doesn't mean He is not present. In the biblical books

Ruth and Esther, God is not directly mentioned, though He is desperately needed. The story of Ruth opens with loss, tragedy and shattered dreams, while Esther tells the story of the near annihilation of God's people. Yet as we read the stories, we see His power at work. He is there. In the same way, there are chapters in our own stories where it seems as if God is silent, even though these are the times when we think we need His voice the most. No words, no dreams, no visions. Only at the chapter's end do we get to see something of the bigger picture, and we discover that He never left our side. He carried us through.

HOW TO PRACTISE IN PAIN

Life happens to all of us. We suffer abuse, we lose loved ones. Our lives veer out of control. We get sick. Our days turn grey. Whatever has happened to us, we get heartsick – and wonder if our relationship with God will make it. How do we move forward? There is no quick fix that solves everything, but there is raw honesty. There is no magic formula, but there is silence and surrender, tears and even joy and freedom. There is prayer and worship, there is God's life-giving Word. There is a Saviour who has known suffering and pain. There is the grace and the power of God.

It's good to know that when life happens to us, God wants to happen to us too. He is with us, God with us – Immanuel.[11] You may not see Him, but He will not leave your side.

6
Practising thanksgiving

Give thanks to the LORD, for he is good;
his love endures forever.
(Psalm 118:1)

Rejoice always, pray continually, give thanks in all circum-
stances, for this is God's will for you in Christ Jesus.
(1 Thessalonians 5:16–18)

THE POWER OF THANKSGIVING

In its first edition for 2009, *Newsweek* magazine compiled a list
of fifty people who together formed a global elite – men and
women who were considered to be the most powerful, most significant (and in a few cases most notorious) people in the world.[1]
According to *Newsweek*, these people would shape our future,
redefine our culture and change our lives. The list contained heads
of state, media moguls and business leaders. And at number 49
was Pastor E. A. Adeboye.

Unknown to many in the Western Church until recently, Pastor
Adeboye is the General Overseer of The Redeemed Christian
Church of God (RCCG), a church born in Lagos, Nigeria. The
RCCG has somewhere in the region of 15,000 branches in Nigeria
alone, but has also established a missionary network of churches
spanning over a hundred countries in both hemispheres.[2]

In 1999, a team from our church in Sheffield visited the
Redeemed Christian Church of God in Lagos. Our trip began
with an amazing, phenomenal, mind-blowing event as we gathered

with hundreds of thousands of believers for a whole night of worship and prayer. We had never seen anything like this. We were eager to discover their secret. We wondered if there was a special method used in their missionary strategy. Perhaps there was a spiritual truth or gift they had received that they could impart to us, that could maybe bring a breakthrough back home in England? Our questions and reflections may have been valid, but it was soon apparent that there was something else we all needed to learn.

Our hosts told us that there were two things they emphasised in their church community: thanksgiving and testimony. We saw it everywhere. It wasn't some artificial, contrived attitude masked in religious language. It was a thankful perspective on life that emanated from everyone we met. People were thankful for their friends, their families. They were thankful for little, everyday, seemingly insignificant things. They were also thankful for hugely significant things – for salvation, miracles and healings. They were thankful for the goodness of God, the kindness of God and the power of God – and their testimonies abounded as an overflow of thanksgiving. One morning I attended a special thanksgiving service, and it was testimony and thanksgiving in motion as men and women danced, laughed, smiled, celebrated, worshipped and prayed. Their thankful hearts produced single-minded lives on fire for Jesus, committed to the gospel. It was wonderful.

It was also such a challenge, to us as a team, but also personally. It was both humbling and inspirational. I realised how much God had given me – friends, job, belongings – that I hadn't even considered thanking Him for. I remembered that time and time again in the name of being 'real' or 'honest', I was easily cynical or sarcastic. Yet this time in Nigeria was inspirational because in the midst of their real lives the people we met had connected with God in reality, and they knew His real power. I was inspired because my heart was hungry; my heart was aching for this.

We faced challenges during our ministry trip that gave us opportunities to learn to be thankful, but it was on our return home that we learned to practise a different perspective on life. For me it began in small ways, looking for things to thank God for, reminding myself that every good and perfect gift came from Him.[3] More challenging was to remain thankful in situations that weren't going my way! But I began to learn. On a corporate level, in response to what we'd learned, our church held Thanksgiving Sundays once a month. Everyone and anyone had the opportunity to share what God had done in their lives. The very fact that these services were being held got you thinking about what you were thankful for that day. The community was ignited by testimonies of healings, of salvation, of comfort in the midst of terrible circumstances, of restoration and blessing. God spoke through our stories. We heard of His mercy, love and faithfulness. Over time (after months of Thanksgiving Sundays), I began to discover that practising thanksgiving had a transforming effect on my heart. The God who touched the lives of my church family, who remembered, who healed and provided, was also my God. And perhaps He would do exactly the same for me.

THANKSGIVING: MORE THAN MINDING YOUR MANNERS!

Saying 'thank you' is a regular feature in our daily conversations. Sometimes we say it to communicate appreciation, feelings of love and gratitude, even relief, in response to what has been done for us. In other situations, 'thank you' conveys some degree of respect and politeness. When we say 'thank you' to the person at the supermarket checkout as they hand us our receipt, it's not usually because we are overcome with joy at the chance to buy groceries, it's just that it's polite! We simply say 'thank you' because it's the right thing to do. It can lead us to thinking that thanksgiving is merely a pleasantry, a good sentiment or an emotional response. Of course, these are all important things, but when it comes to the issue of the heart, practising thanksgiving amounts to more than minding our manners and saying the right words. In our journey with God, thanksgiving has the potential to be a heart- and life-transforming tangible force to be reckoned with.

When we thank God, we're simply recognising the greatness of God and responding to the goodness of God in our lives. As those thankful thoughts and attitudes take shape and find words, they become testimony. And those testimonies, recollections of God's goodness and greatness in action, act like signposts to our heart (and the hearts of others), showing us which direction we need to follow.

The message of the gospel is incredible: God, who knew us yet loved us, sent His Son to die for us, that we might know Him. Yet sometimes it's all too familiar to us, particularly if we live in a culture with Christendom in its history. We celebrate Christian festivals, Christian symbols, churches; crosses are commonplace in our towns and cities. Christendom has been our religious wall-paper, and we can simply forget how amazing Jesus is. It's not that we forget what He's done, but we often forget the signifi-cance of the cross, the implications of a life without the cross. We forget the price that He paid, for our peace with God. 'Saviour' is just a term, rather than the reality of what He has done for us. We can take the power of God for granted; we fail to recognise His provision demonstrated by an incredible sunrise, the rain that soaks the land, and the stars that illuminate the night-time expanse. It's just the sun, the rain, the sky. Practising thanksgiving helps us actively to remember who God is. When we don't actively remember, we too easily forget.

There is a pattern throughout the Old Testament, that when God's people forgot who He was and what He had done for them, they drifted from Him. They forgot that He loved them, and they chose to worship other gods or make some of their own. They forgot that He was their provider, their strength, and they looked to the strength of their armies and demanded a king like the countries around them. We see God raising up leaders, judges, kings, priests and prophets to call people back to Himself and to remind them of what He had done for them in Egypt, the Red Sea, in countless testimonies of God's power and love. These leaders called people actively to remember, in songs, in words, in physical actions.

The same pattern can be true for each one of us. When we forget what God has done for us, personally, for our families, for our church, we too can drift in our commitment to Him. We might forget the story of His love for us and choose to put other ideas or people first in our lives. We might forget that God is our strength and provider, and depend too much on our own resources or on other people in our lives to meet our needs and desires. We might become cynical.

The solution for God's people then is the same for God's people now. We need actively to remember God's goodness and greatness through thanksgiving and testimony. Thanksgiving is a relentless and powerful force in spiritual warfare. Our enemy, the one whom Jesus describes as a thief who comes to steal, kill and destroy,[4] actively seeks to undermine our confidence in God's goodness and greatness. He wants to steal our hope in God, kill our love and destroy our relationship with Him. He wants to twist our perspective on the wonderful things we have in life and ascribe them to our own abilities so that we think we don't need God. He wants to take our disappointments and difficulties and convince us that God is not worth following. Testimony clearly has a role to play in overcoming the enemy's schemes:

They triumphed over him
by the blood of the Lamb
and by the word of their testimony;
they did not love their lives so much
as to shrink from death.[5]

When we are reminded of the goodness and greatness of God in our lives, we are encouraged to reach for Him and rely on Him again. We have fresh perspective on our lives; our faith is built up; our confidence in God grows. Our stories of God's goodness and greatness remind us that the God who came through for us in the past will do so again.

LESSONS FROM A THANKFUL PEOPLE

Paul's letter to the Philippian Christians is described by some theologians as Paul's happiest letter.

It's a remarkable letter anyway, full of encouragement and guidance. But when we consider Paul's circumstances and those of the Philippians when this letter was written, the remarkable becomes radical. Paul did not write this from a cozy armchair, but from a primitive prison, as he waited to find out whether his imprisonment would result in his death. Before he met Jesus, he was a bright and rising star in the Jewish religious community. He was one to watch. After he met Jesus, his life was forever changed. He became the enemy of those who were once his friends, and also of the Roman Empire. For the sake of the gospel, Paul experienced death threats and assassination attempts, beatings with rods and lashes, shipwrecks, prison sentences, hunger and starvation. The missionary churches and church plants had successes, but also frustrations and failures. He could have been forgiven for wondering if it was worth it.

The Philippian Christians were not in a comfortable position either. Philippi was a Roman colony, a place of many religious practices including the cult of the emperor, meaning that whoever ruled the Roman Empire at that time was seen as a god. So when the Philippian church sang that Jesus was Lord, it was not just offensive, it was treason. Traitors to the Roman Empire were not welcome. The Philippians suffered great persecution because they loved Jesus. Following Jesus also cost them socially and professionally. To function in a place like Philippi required joining various societies that involved worshipping someone other than God. As a result, their businesses were affected. In 2 Corinthians Paul describes the Philippian church as suffering deep poverty.

When Paul writes this letter, the Philippian Christians were going through tough times as a church family. They had many great things going for them. For example, in spite of their poverty, they were incredibly generous, supporting Paul as he served and planted churches elsewhere. However, relationships were strained. There were some significant relationship breakdowns between key leaders. There were differing theological views that threatened to divide the church. The Philippian church felt under pressure both internally and externally.

And yet, into this crucible of pressure and persecution for all concerned, Paul writes these words:

> Always be full of joy in the Lord. I say it again – rejoice! Let everyone see that you are considerate in all you do. Remember, the Lord is coming soon.
>
> Don't worry about anything; instead, pray about everything. Tell God what you need, and thank him for all he has done. Then you will experience God's peace, which exceeds anything we can understand. His peace will guard your hearts and minds as you live in Christ Jesus.
>
> And now, dear brothers and sisters, one final thing. Fix your

thoughts on what is true, and honourable, and right, and pure, and lovely, and admirable. Think about things that are excellent and worthy of praise.[6]

Wow. Just wow. How challenging are these words as we discover their context?

Maybe the last thing we feel like doing is being thankful. We feel pressure and pain and vulnerability as we go through some very real difficulties. These verses are not only a powerful reminder that practising thanksgiving is not just for the good times or the good feelings, but they also give us some great tips on practising thanksgiving and cultivating a thankful heart, in the best and worst of times.

GET YOUR PRAISE ON!

Always be full of joy in the Lord. I say it again – rejoice![7]

Paul encourages the Philippians to rejoice. He calls them to celebrate God, to remind themselves of His goodness and greatness. Praise and worship are great ways to practise thanksgiving and cultivate a thankful heart. In Psalm 100:4 the psalmist encourages God's people to enter the gates of God's temple with thanksgiving, to enter His courts with praise. The style of praise and worship is not the issue; it's the heart that matters. Praise doesn't have to be sung: we can speak it out, shout it out. I love watching my girls get excited, especially around birthdays. Their 'thank yous' have ranged from hugs, kisses and squeals of giddiness to awe and silence followed by jumping up and down! Paul is encouraging us to rejoice before our heavenly Father.

When were we last full of joy because we have Jesus in our life? Sometimes that is a feeling, but we know for Paul and the

Philippians it was not about feelings. Paul is saying: in these pressures, choose to rejoice in God, focus on Him for perspective rather than on your opinions or feelings. We remind ourselves of His greatness as we reflect on His character. We can speak out the names of God, the Bible verses that describe God, to remind ourselves of His timeless nature: Saviour, Healer, Creator, Deliverer, Holy, Almighty God, Prince of Peace, Father. As we speak or sing out His name and His nature, it reminds our hearts that this God *is our God*. He is the same, yesterday, today and for ever, and that applies to our lives too.

Paul simply won't let it go: 'I say it again – rejoice!' It's not surprising when you consider Paul's spiritual and cultural heritage. Through biblical history we see that God's people had a pattern of feasts, festivals, holy days and pilgrimage. Remembering God's goodness and greatness was not purely cerebral; it encompassed every area of life. There were feasts which marked times of God's intervention on behalf of His people. The feast of Unleavened Bread began with the Passover, a specific meal that recalled God's deliverance of His people from Egypt, then continued with seven days of gatherings, eating special food, remembering the miracle of the exodus. The feast of Purim, in remembrance of God's deliverance in the time of Esther, involved feasting on good food and drink and giving presents. The feast of Tabernacles remembered the journey from Egypt to Canaan, with feasts and camping in booths to remember where God's people had once been. There were feasts to remember God's provision, to thank Him for the harvest times. Imagine what it must have been like, celebrating the Passover and the feast of Unleavened Bread just a few years after the exodus. Imagine the response when the question 'What does this ceremony mean to you?' was asked during the Passover meal. Can you hear the silence as people tried to find the words to say what God meant to them now? Or can you hear the tears and the laughter of a liberated people? Imagine the scenes at the first festival of Purim, as God's people celebrated that the God of the exodus had delivered them again. Imagine the gifts they would have shared, the food they would have eaten to celebrate the gift of life they had been given. Imagine the party they would have had! And why not? These were good times that reminded people of a good God! They were visible expressions of His kindness, tangible symbols of His love, recollections of His power.

PRACTISING THANKSGIVING – GOOD TIMES WITH A GOOD GOD!

When we celebrate God in a practical way – around a meal, a party, shared stories – it helps us to remember Him in everyday life. We too have festivals that can act as a springboard to celebrating God's goodness. Since we've moved to the USA, we've started to celebrate Thanksgiving. Thanksgiving is a harvest festival, historically giving thanks for good crops, but in the USA it also commemorates a meal the Pilgrims shared with the Native American community who had taught them how to plant crops and hunt. Now, like any other national holiday or religious festival, it can be an opportunity to overeat and drink, and shop! But equally, like any other national holiday, it can be a time when we can choose to connect with God at a deeper level. Thanksgiving offers us a perfect opportunity to practise thanksgiving in an everyday, memorable way. We get together with friends and eat great food, but we also make a point of sharing testimonies around the table, and we tell people how thankful we are for them. Everyone is included, of any age or stage in life.

My favourite Thanksgiving took place last year at our church. We ran an Alpha course (an informal course aimed at introducing people to the basics of the Christian faith) and it ended around the Thanksgiving season. Every week our time began with a meal, and everyone agreed that we should make our final meal a big Thanksgiving dinner. This was no ordinary pot-luck church supper. The food was amazing; everybody brought some traditional Thanksgiving fare. Somehow I find it easier to worship God passionately when I can smell a good roast dinner in the background! During the meal, we had an open mic where anyone and everyone could share what God had done. The stories began with wonderful testimonies of what God had done during the Alpha course: freedom, healing, salvation – I never get bored of hearing about that. The testimonies broadened as people shared what God had done in their lives over the years. For me, the most poignant moment was when one of the older members of the church family read a poem he'd written for his wife of over forty years. She'd had a stroke a few years previously, and he too was frail, but they were as active as they could be in the life of the church. It was moving to listen to him publicly thank God for her and to see her response, and a reminder of how God strengthens and sustains our marriages and families.

I left church that night full not just physically, but also full of the joy of the Lord, amazed that our God, so mighty, was still so interested and so active in our everyday lives.

Q. How do we celebrate God's goodness and greatness in our lives? How could this redefine Christmas, Easter and Pentecost?

Could we take some time – even some time off – to celebrate our story with God? We have birthday parties: so we could celebrate the day we met Jesus, or a significant event that He brought us through. What could it be like, to take the time to have some fun, eat good food and simply tell our families and friends how good our God is? Maybe our stories would be told through tears or laughter too as we remember what God has done.

TRADING YOUR ANXIETIES FOR THANKSGIVING

Let your gentleness be evident to all. The Lord is near. Do not be anxious about anything, but in every situation, by prayer and petition, with thanksgiving, present your requests to God.[8]

After an encouragement towards godly attitudes in relationships, Paul guides the Philippian community to trade their anxieties for prayer and thanksgiving. He says something similar to the Thessalonian church, another persecuted community:[9]

Rejoice always, pray continually, give thanks in all circumstances; for this is God's will for you in Christ Jesus.[10]

Considering the pressure the persecuted Christians were under, it makes sense that Paul gives the churches a way to deal with anxiety. It's still salient advice today. Though the reasons may differ, we've all known struggles with anxiety. We get anxious about our lives, our health, those we love, what's happening at church or work. Yet, left unattended, anxiety has an erosive effect on our lives. It affects our daily decisions, how we eat and drink, how we speak, how we spend. It harasses us at night as we toss and turn, thinking ourselves in and out of oblivion and disaster. Anxiety wears down relationships and can even affect our health. And as it erodes our confidence in God's goodness and greatness, it begins to shape our journey with God, isolating us from Him, even leading us in a different direction.

Paul's words are an encouragement to bring the situations that make us anxious before God in prayer. Nothing is too small or insignificant for us to talk to God about, and we need His guidance and wisdom in those situations. Furthermore, He invites them (and us) to do so with thanksgiving. It's important to note that in these verses Paul doesn't call Christians to rejoice and be thankful *for* everything. There are some great things in life for which we are thankful, and rightly so. But there are also some awful things that have happened. He is not pretending that the bad times are actually good – that would be denial. The invitation here is to choose to be thankful *in* every circumstance. There's an important distinction between the two ideas; it's not a play on words which underneath mean the same thing. Paul's prison sentence and constant persecution was not good, but Paul was certain that his God was. His God was bigger than any prison sentence. God might save Paul this time, but even if He didn't, Paul's thankful, rejoicing heart knew that his life had not been wasted on living for Jesus. This attitude of gratitude permeated his life.

We aren't powerful enough to rid ourselves of the anxieties that confuse and isolate us from God. However, our choice to pray and be thankful is an active step away from anxiety. When we give thanks *in* all circumstances, we choose to remind ourselves of God's goodness in every part of our lives. We remind ourselves of how He's answered prayers in the past, we remind ourselves of His character. Then we allow those reminders to shape our perspective on our current needs and prayer requests. Instead of anxiety and isolation, we're reconnected with the living God and His resources.

It can still be a challenge, though, because thanksgiving is often the last thing we feel like doing when life is overwhelming. We've already seen that worship and celebration can transform our perspective. Sometimes it helps to find other creative ways to trade our anxieties for thanksgiving.

RAISE YOUR EBENEZER!

Then Samuel took a stone and set it up between Mizpah and Shen. He named it Ebenezer, saying, 'Thus far the LORD has helped us.'

So the Philistines were subdued and they stopped invading Israel's territory. Throughout Samuel's lifetime, the hand of the LORD was against the Philistines.[11]

Samuel was the last great judge of Israel. He was a mediator between God and His people, calling God's people to be faithful to Him and speaking to God on their behalf. After a period when the people chose to worship other gods, Samuel calls the people to Mizpah to pray, repent and renew their commitment to God (1 Samuel 7). However, their enemies the Philistines are watching. The Israelites are gathered in one place, and though Samuel is the judge of Israel, the Israelites don't have a king, a symbol of strength and power, like the other nations. They are vulnerable. The Philistines see this as a prime opportunity and attack the people of Israel. What the Philistines don't see is that the Israelites have no king because the Lord is their king. He is the source of their strength and power, and He intervenes to defeat the Philistines.

After the battle has been won, Samuel sets up an *Ebenezer*, or 'stone of help'. Future generations travelling between Mizpah and Shen would see this stone, the symbol of God's goodness and power at work among His people – a reminder that Israel's God was stronger than the might of the nations.

We need our Ebenezers to help us practise thanksgiving in all circumstances. We need reminders of when the Lord has helped us. Perhaps it's a little impractical to build a stone monument, but we can be creative in other ways. We can have an 'Ebenezer list' on a sheet of paper, with a list of the occasions when God has intervened on our behalf. We can leave the list anywhere and everywhere: in our Bibles, in our purses, on our desk, on our refrigerator. Then, when the struggles come and it's hard to pray or even think of God's faithfulness, our Ebenezer list is there to encourage us.

Perhaps you can build an Ebenezer with your community. A number of our closest friends whom we've known for years moved away from Phoenix recently. We're part of a missional order and moved from the UK to the USA together as a missionary team. More than that, we're an extended family. Our Phoenix experience has been difficult at times, but God has been good to us. One night we drove into the Arizona desert and worshipped God together. Then we built our Ebenezer. As each person gave thanks, a rock was added to the pile, until our 'monument' was built. In the morning it would have looked pretty meaningless to any passing coyote or rattlesnake or hiker, but to us it was the symbol of the goodness of God in the desert.

My favourite way of giving thanks in all circumstances is a practice my husband and I started a couple of years ago, called the 'Family Ebenezer'. It's a way to remember all the good things the Lord has done for us throughout the year. Every year, as Thanksgiving draws near, we buy a large, deep photo frame that looks a bit like a box with a glass door. We fill it with memories of people, events and opportunities that the Lord has provided for us throughout the year, and we mount it on a wall. Every time we pass the wall of Ebenezers, we're reminded of what God has done and we have another chance to be thankful. Whenever we lose sight of God's faithfulness, whenever we worry about our lives or our kids, we have a place to go to remember that God is good and He has not forgotten us. There's a dollar bill in each box, reminding us of God's constant provision over the years. There are family photos, and pictures of places and people who were special to our family that year. There are Bible verses and lines of worship songs that have helped us through the year. Zoë's ultra-sound picture is there. There's the card Chris gave me after my dad died. Sometimes the thanksgiving comes with tears. But it's our family monument, our stone of help. There are days when I go to our Ebenezers and speak out all the things God has done for us, illustrated on our wall. It's an amazing faith-building experience, it cultivates a grateful heart and it makes me smile. It reminds me not to take for granted the blessing of my husband, my kids and everything and everyone else I have. There are other days when I've leaned against the wall in tears because I'm struggling or afraid. My prayer then is, 'Lord, you've been good before. I know you'll be good to us again. Thank you . . .' Now, as we go through the year, we pick up things for the Ebenezer. It helps us develop a thankful heart throughout the year.

A FEW FINAL THOUGHTS

Then you will experience God's peace, which exceeds anything we can understand. His peace will guard your hearts and minds as you live in Christ Jesus.

And now, dear brothers and sisters, one final thing. Fix your thoughts on what is true, and honourable, and right, and pure, and lovely, and admirable. Think about things that are excellent and worthy of praise.[12]

No one would have blamed Paul for being miserable as he languished in that prison cell. Yet Paul's happiest letter communicates a joy and security that simply doesn't make human sense when you look at the life he has led. He had a different approach: his imprisonments were where some of the New Testament was written, and some of those around him met the Lord.[13] In the same way, the Philippians were under immense pressure. They could have just given up, worshipped the emperor and got their jobs back rather than endure the crippling poverty. They could have allowed their differences to destroy them rather than cause them to lean on God. But instead this church sponsored Paul's mission trips, looked after his team and was generous and sacrificial in order to see more people meet Jesus. He was still worth it.

How did they do it? How did they manage to rise above their circumstances and keep pursuing God so fervently? They did it with God's help! When we connect with God's resources, we don't do it, God does. The specific resource Paul speaks of here is *peace*, which is not merely the absence of worry, but something given to us from Jesus by His Spirit.[14] When we receive peace we experience a God-given calm, a God-given security, even a God-given comfort in the face of answers that we cannot find and circumstances we cannot control. When I walk away from our Ebenezer, my circumstances may be exactly the same, but God's peace transforms my perspective and calms me. Some days are easier than others; it can be a battle being thankful when all my frustrations rise to the surface! Still, even in those times, it's an opportunity to talk with God about what's in my heart and ask Him to meet with me. When we practise thanksgiving, we fix our minds on good things; we fix our minds on truth, on things that are pure and praiseworthy.

The responses to tough times shown by Paul and the Philippian community exemplify this principle. They fixed their minds on the good things, on the truth. As a result, Paul's letter overflows with God-given encouragement and insight and the Philippians overflowed with missionary passion and generosity. We too need to choose to fix our minds on the truth – on God's goodness and greatness. What our minds focus on in these moments will determine how and what we believe and ultimately how we live. If we focus on despair and anxiety, we can end up feeling hopeless and cynical, making choices outside our relationship with God, because there seems no point in trusting Him. Instead, we need to bring our despair and hopelessness, our anxiety and cynicism, to God. Then we can lay them down at the cross and trade them for thanksgiving. When we focus on God's goodness and greatness, it transforms and renews our minds. We know that we can hold on to Him, and we know that He's worth pursuing with every part of our lives.

As Paul suggests, let us imitate his example,[15] and choose thankfulness. Choose to rejoice and celebrate. Choose to pray and give thanks in all circumstances. Like Paul, let's choose to rely on God's resources rather than our own, and fix our minds on the truth.

Raise your Ebenezer and practise thanksgiving.

> Come Thou Fount of every blessing
> Tune my heart to sing Thy grace;
> Streams of mercy, never ceasing,
> Call for songs of loudest praise.
> Teach me some melodious sonnet,
> Sung by flaming tongues above.
> Praise the mount! I'm fixed upon it,
> Mount of God's unchanging love.
>
> Here I raise my Ebenezer;
> Hither by Thy help I'm come;
> And I hope, by Thy good pleasure,
> Safely to arrive at home.
> Jesus sought me when a stranger,
> Wandering from the fold of God;
> He, to rescue me from danger,
> Interposed His precious blood.

O to grace how great a debtor
Daily I'm constrained to be!
Let that grace now like a fetter,
Bind my wandering heart to Thee.
Prone to wander, Lord, I feel it,
Prone to leave the God I love;
Here's my heart, O take and seal it,
Seal it for Thy courts above.[16]

*   *   *

INTRODUCING SECTION TWO

When we give God access to our hearts, we are changed. How do we respond to His love and power? We follow Jesus, the One who has given us forgiveness, freedom and healing. To follow means much more than to show the appreciation given by a fan. It means we shape our lives in the light of His example. We make His priorities our priorities. The chapters in Section Two seek to explore these priorities as we train ourselves to be godly.

'Deserts and shipwrecks' and 'Connecting with God' look *up*, exploring how we develop our relationship with God the Father.

'The life together – a glimpse of His glory' and 'Sometimes you can't make it on your own' look *in* at our relationships with other believers.

Finally, 'A walk across the park' and 'Lifesaver' look *out*, investigating how we can attend to our relationship with the world around.

SECTION TWO
Practising Life

7
Deserts and shipwrecks

Be still, and know that I am God.
(Psalm 46:10)

INTO THE DESERT

The Acts of the Apostles tells the story of the birth of the Christian Church. Alongside stories of missionary journeys, apostolic endeavours and miraculous signs and wonders is the story of a church that would encounter opposition and even violence in the name of following Christ. For three hundred years, the early church endured periodic bouts of persecution at the hands of the Roman authorities. In some cases the persecution was localised; at other times it was an empire-wide directive given by the Roman government.

Most of us can only imagine the suffering that our Christian ancestors experienced as they lived on the edges of society, under a very real threat. During these periods of persecution, churches were razed to the ground, Christian books were burned. Christians were harassed and abused, their careers stalled because of their commitment to Christ. Men and women were imprisoned, tortured and killed.

Then, in AD 313, their world changed. Constantine and Licinius issued the Edict of Milan which proclaimed religious tolerance throughout the Roman Empire. It was the birth of a new day, a brand-new era. It changed everything. The great persecution of

Diocletian's rule was over, and Christians were being restored. They received back property that had been confiscated, and worship gatherings were now legal. Exposed to Christianity as a child, the Roman Emperor Constantine declared himself a Christian in his forties, crediting God with his successes.

Constantine became the Church's patron. Under his rule, the once-persecuted churches became wealthy landowners. Clergy received new privileges, and Christians rose to positions of power and influence within the Empire. After years on the edge, under the threat of persecution, finally these faithful outcasts had been given a legitimate voice. Perhaps this could be an opportunity for influence, a chance to communicate the gospel throughout the Empire, to usher in their Saviour's return. It was more complex than that, however. As is always the case for Christians, power and privilege presented both an opportunity and a cost. In this new era, Christianity was culturally acceptable and popular, perhaps even a way to advance professionally.

Not everyone felt comfortable about the new-found popularity. It was unsettling. Once persecution was the great threat; now it appeared that wealth, respectability and comfort posed a threat of their own to the Christians. Would they remain faithful in the good times? What did it mean to be a Christian anyway? Was it a social club, a source of professional advancement? How did this affect moral values? Was Christianity just the 'in' thing?

There were many responses to the birth of a new day and new way. While some Christians embraced the political and social opportunities, others simply walked away from the popular choice and the privilege to live a different way. They walked away from the cities and into the desert. Christians like Anthony (c. 251–356), a wealthy Egyptian Christian in Alexandria. Anthony heard the gospel being read in church and, upon hearing Jesus' words to the rich young ruler – "'One thing you lack," he said. "Go, sell everything you have and give to the poor, and you will have treasure in heaven. Then come, follow me"[1] – he responded literally. Anthony sold or gave away all his possessions and property and pursued a new life of solitude in the desert. There were others, like Syncletica, known to be a wealthy and beautiful woman, who left a life of privilege in the city and, with her sister, lived in a crypt as a hermit. The desert saints saw the dangers of buying into the glamour and prestige of society. They didn't want or need to fit, in fact they needed to ensure that they didn't water themselves down to fit. The life of solitude reflected their desire to pull away from worldly distractions. Thomas Merton (a twentieth-century monk) said that these desert saints saw society as a shipwreck where every person had to swim for their lives. They believed that 'to let oneself drift along, passively accepting the tenets and values of what they knew as society, was purely and simply a disaster'.[2]

The desert life was also undertaken to pursue obedience and surrender to God at a deeper level. They were not going to settle for a comfortable Christianity on a shipwreck. The desert fathers and mothers adopted practices of prayer and silence which ensured that they would not be dragged into the shallow values of the world around them. There in the isolation, like the examples of Jesus and Paul, the desert was the place to grapple with the issues and temptations of the human heart. It was also the place where the desert saints encountered spiritual transformation and power. Many people were drawn to men and women like these, learning from their practices and seeking the spiritual wisdom and power received from their life in the desert.

TWENTY-FIRST-CENTURY SHIPWRECK

How do we respond to society today, a twenty-first-century shipwreck? In my former years, swimming away from the shipwreck seemed a lot more obvious. It meant being the sober one in the company of merry friends. It was the no-sex-please-I'm-a-single-Christian attitude, or the yes-I-did-just-say-I-was-going-to-church-tonight statement. Today, reflecting on Merton's observations of the desert fathers and mothers, I have to ask myself if I still notice that society is a shipwreck. Do I truly know that its values and aspirations cannot give me stability or safety? Or do I gently, imperceptibly, absorb what society suggests about money, power, beauty, worth, relationships, even Jesus? What defines how I relate to my friends and family – the Bible or a magazine? What determines my work ethic? Or, frankly, my ethics, period? The honest answer is that sometimes it's hard to tell, which is why I really need to get away from it all somehow. It helps me see things clearly.

In the West, we live in a society that has been shaped by Christian values. Christianity is still considered to be the dominant cultural influence, even in Western cultures where that influence is waning. Perhaps we need to reflect on the conditions to which the desert saints responded. They responded to a world where Christianity was culturally acceptable, even politically beneficial. It was a world where, in their opinion, privilege and power endangered a genuine commitment to Christ. Their perspective offers a salient challenge to the twenty-first-century Western Christian. How do we respond in our relative comfort? Do we need to pay close attention in case comfort becomes passivity, or cultural relevance becomes compromise? Instead of ringing out like a radical prophetic voice, Christianity can become a pleasant, respectable thing to do and be, a bit like being a good citizen. Like the desert saints, we need something more than casual Christianity. Perhaps we too need to develop practices that help us steal away from the frenetic pace of life and connect with God at a deep level, a heart-shaping, life-transforming level. Without such practices, we're drifting along on stormy seas, with only a shipwreck for safety. Our lives look very different from those of the desert saints in the third to fifth centuries AD. But there is something powerful and challenging we can learn from their example as we seek to follow God in everyday life. It was integral to their spirituality that their lives were not only sharply distinct from the world around them, but also deeply connected to God. We may not have the austerity of the desert, but there are a number of things we can do to apply those same principles in our world.

TAKE A LONG, HARD LOOK AT YOUR LIFE

The desert saints took a long, hard look at how Christianity was changing in their brave new world, and then they took decisive steps. When the apostle Paul advises Timothy to 'train yourself to be godly',[3] he encourages his protégé:

> Watch your life and doctrine closely. Persevere in them, because if you do, you will save both yourself and your hearers.[4]

Fundamental to Timothy's 'godliness training' was practising observation – watching. Paul encouraged Timothy to take a long, hard look at his life and a long, hard look at what he taught. Together, these observations would indicate what the young leader truly believed in. And then Paul advises Timothy to persevere in this practice: 'just keep at it', as *The Message* translation puts it, so that 'you and those who hear you will experience salvation'. Paul calls Timothy to take responsibility, to be intentional in both his relationship with God and his calling.

Paul's encouragement to take a long, hard look at life extends to us today. How comfortable would it be to spend a day paying close attention to every aspect of how we live? Perhaps we'd hear the words we said to that driver who nearly crashed into us. We'd remember the thoughts that went through our minds, the positive ones, the negative ones, the judgmental, critical ones. We'd look at how we related to our friends and our family that day. Was that a hint of selfishness and resentment in that phone conversation? Did we make time to be with those we love, or are we consumed with our work, our TV show, our computer? We might think of how stress or boredom dictated what we ate, or how much we had to drink. Were we conscious of God's presence, guidance, His mere existence, today?

We may not be in Timothy's position of teaching a church community, but there is something in the principle of paying attention to what we say about our understanding of God, watching our doctrine. What do we believe in? And what has shaped those beliefs? We're learning all the time, being taught all the time. We're taught by society's values and opinions, by talk-show hosts and their experts, by columnists. We're shaped by our personal experiences, good and bad. All these things affect what we believe. As we take a long, hard look, we might discover that our thoughts on money are shaped by what society thinks. We might notice a relationship that remains broken, but we can't get our head around the Bible's view on forgiveness, so we've made a notable exception for that person!

Taking a long, hard look is not a comfortable thing to do. It's time consuming, and it can be intense. Yet, as Paul indicates to Timothy, it makes all the difference to our lives and to those around us. It is an opportunity to swim away from the shipwreck; a chance to trade Christianity Lite for the depth of the desert.

A LIFE AUDIT

We're used to parent-teacher conferences which review how our kids are doing at school; we're used to professional reviews at work. How about a review of how we're doing with God?

A number of years ago, I began to explore a way of watching my life and beliefs more closely and began an annual review, between Christmas and New Year. I love making New Year's resolutions, and wanted to take the time to look to the coming year with God. There were a number of areas in my life I wanted to review. I looked at my friendships, my finances, my health, my relationship with men, my career. Then I looked at how I felt about my church and my relationship with God.

I bought a notebook and gave each topic a couple of pages. I listed all the positives of the year on one side and the negatives on the other, looking for any 'stand-out' moments or patterns of behaviour, observing how I felt. It wasn't a rushed process, and sometimes it was interrupted by prayers, confessions, even lunch! The aim was to make space for God through the entire process.

Eventually I had all my highs and lows of the year there for me to see. I could see how they had affected me. Before my eyes I saw the records of great breakthroughs and huge disappointments. I saw the areas of my life which remained unresolved and confused. I could see the relationships that were working well and the ones which still brought about some kind of reaction in me. A close look at my life revealed my hopes, attitudes and habits, things I barely noticed in the everyday bustle.

Then I looked more specifically at my relationship with God. How was my prayer life? What worked, and what failed? Were there any major prayers answered? How did I approach the Bible? Were there any good books I'd read? Had I shared my faith, seen anyone come to the Lord that year? Was it a year of trusting God, or holding back? And why?

These life audits were arduous, but significant. They forced me to do something I was avoiding: they forced me to stop and look; stop and praise; stop and confess; stop and address certain inconsistencies in my life. The life audits helped me connect what I believed to what was happening in my life. For example, as I struggled with being single and feeling lonely, I could see how my faith was being eroded by this particular storm. I could see patterns of temptation where I was drawn to the wreckage of a sinking ship.

This wasn't a performance exercise, to see whether I'd been a good A-grade Christian in all areas. It was to see where I was really at, and to start working through it with God. The process ended with prayer over each subject. I'd pray and listen for a verse of Scripture that would be my guide for the year ahead. I would pray for God to speak to me and lead me. I'd write down the verses that came to mind, or anything that I felt God might be communicating to me. The notebook was a helpful reference point throughout the year.

As a married woman with two young children, the Christmas season is no longer the best time to do this kind of review. I'm busy playing with new toys and being Christmassy! These days I find that the season of Lent is a helpful time for me to dedicate to reviewing. I find a fixed period helpful, and I love the idea of going into the desert as the Church marks the time Jesus spent in the wilderness.

The subjects I review have changed. My review is less ambitious, I've narrowed down the topics and now I probably review things more than once a year. Yet the principle of taking a long, hard look is the same.

GETTING STARTED

How could you watch your life and beliefs more closely? What areas of your life are in need of a review? How regularly would you like to review? Here are some suggestions to help get you started.

Something to try – a 'life review'

- You'll need a notebook, a pen and a Bible.
- Decide how long a period you wish to review – a year, a term, a month.
- Start with a few topics.
- Arrange some time on your own, or with a close friend – where you can't be interrupted. Turn off the mobile and get off the Internet!
- Pray as you begin your review.
- Record your significant moments of the year, both the highs and the lows.
- Don't rush it!
- Pray over each topic. Pause for a moment, listen to God and see if there are any scriptural verses that specifically come to mind as guidance for the way ahead. (Don't worry if you don't get verses.)

Remember, it's a long, hard look, not a performance. It doesn't have to be completed in one sitting; take time over it. Time is something that we seem to have little of in the Western world – time to watch and look, time to think and feel, time to stop. Yet it's exactly what we need as human beings, time to rest and regenerate. For us as believers, it's critical. We need to learn how to give ourselves space to go deeper with God. One very simple way of doing that is by resting, having some time *off*. Who would have thought that rest could be a spiritual practice? Well, actually, God did. God does.

SWIMMING IN THE OPPOSITE DIRECTION

The desert saints took a long, hard look . . . and turned in the opposite direction. Instead of wealth and popularity, they chose the desert. Instead of clinging to the shipwreck, they swam in the opposite direction, clinging on to the life they were calling people to live. There are so many parallels we could make as we respond to our twenty-first-century situation, many ways to swim against the tide. But as we explore our spiritual growth and maturity in everyday life, perhaps one thing is worthy of particular mention.

In his book *The Story of Christian Spirituality*, spanning two thousand years of Christianity across the globe, Gordon Mursell (Bishop of Stafford) ponders Christianity's twenty-first-century challenges. Reflecting on the insights that the Bible and Christian tradition have to offer Christians in a fast-paced, ever-changing world, he highlights the need for taking a day of rest.

> The day on which God paused for breath is an enduring reminder to us that we are made for more than work. We are made for worship, for play, for childlike wonder, for a constant experience of renewal and recreation, for a right balance between activity and rest.[5]

Why would rest be so crucial, so fundamental? Taking a day off seems practical and healthy, but how is it *spiritual?* Who sees it as spiritual?

God does. He places a high priority on rest. So much so, that when humanity is created on the sixth day, rest is their first experience on the seventh! No striving to please God and earn the Creator's approval and affections; just rest. And later, when God writes the Ten Commandments, not only does the Sabbath make the top ten, it's number four. God is committed to resting! Even in Jesus' ministry, when amazing things are happening and it seems the perfect time and conditions to work, serve and minister, Jesus takes the disciples away to retreat and rest.[6]

In stark contrast, our society seems to find it impossible to switch off. It expresses itself in many ways. It might be long hours at work, followed by long hours of reading and responding to the emails that arrive on our phones. It expresses itself in the compelling desire to have our children involved in every possible activity, all to a high standard, without questioning the cost to the family unit or the child. It's seen in the multi-tasking gone mad as we Facebook, Twitter and Skype with our virtual community, while we work, study or attend to tasks around the home. It's not a life that's full; it's a life that's too full, without ever asking the question, 'Why?' Is there an emptiness inside that we're trying to fill so badly that we simply cannot stop and switch off?

We might wonder if such activity is a bad thing; after all, it's just keeping busy. Except that it violates the way we're designed. In the end something has to give. It's like trying to drive a car at seventy-five miles an hour in first gear. Eventually, something is going to get damaged and burn out. Something or someone. People get burned out, they succumb to illnesses which are avoidable or the direct result of stress and anxiety. And people escape into extremes for some relief.

Have we twenty-first-century Christians turned away from that way of doing things? Or do we live to the world's rhythms, with the added commitment of church ministry things to do too? Perhaps we work so hard, and so dutifully, that we call our over-work 'passion' and 'commitment', instead of disobedience. Maybe I sound melodramatic, but a closer look might show us why this is so important.

WHY DOES IT MATTER?

Perhaps you are wondering what having a day off has to do with a devotional life, with spiritual formation. Scripture doesn't compartmentalise our spirituality. Spirituality is holistic. When we rest, we are renewed to face another day. We have space to think, to breathe, to recover, to grieve. When we step off life's treadmill, we get to see life more clearly and hopefully enjoy what's truly important. We manage to switch off. Our mind, heart, body and spirit, all inextricably linked anyway, have a chance to regenerate when we relax. So when we push ourselves too hard by doing too much, our mind and emotions become cluttered and overstimulated, and our receptivity to God is affected too. It's not because we've suddenly become hard-hearted, but there just isn't the time or the energy to invest creatively in yet another thing.

The desert saints understood that to adopt the culture's pattern wholesale, without critique, was costly.

'YOU CAN'T CHEAT THE SABBATH'

A number of years ago, Steve Nicholson, a Vineyard church pastor from the USA, came to spend time with our church's leadership team, teaching and mentoring us. I was eager to glean all I could from him; after all, he'd seen and done so much. We were a bunch of passionate young leaders, ready to take on the city, if not the world. I'm not sure what I was expecting to hear, maybe church planting stories, that sort of thing. But that was not what he came to say to us that night. In straightforward, assured tones, he said, 'You can't cheat the Sabbath.'

He went on to say that when we're overworked and overtired, we don't even realise it initially because we're running on adrenalin, but eventually it all catches up and we make decisions as though we were drunk, erratic, impulsive, out of control.

You can't cheat the Sabbath.

When we're overtired, a number of things can happen. We can make decisions too quickly, because we're frustrated and don't have the energy. Our words are harsher, blunter, more indiscreet. We say things we should regret, but don't in the moment. Temptation can be much more compelling and often a lot harder to resist. Our defences are down, our motivation subdued. And so we make bad choices, ignoring our vulnerability at our peril.

I remember one particular Christmas shopping trip at the end of an exhausting few months at work. I'd had heartburn daily, I felt perpetually run down. My roommate, who was a nurse, had tried to point out that my pace of life was madness, but I always had an answer for why. No one was overworking me; I was at a church that took the biblical principles of rest seriously. What was going on was internal. I busied myself to avoid the pain I felt at the time about being single. If I was working, I didn't have to deal with the fact that friends were on dates; I didn't have to consider my insecurities, because I didn't leave a spare moment for them to sneak up and bite me. I worked long hours in a bid to prove my godliness and my value, to God, to others, to myself. Yet there I was in pain, empty, feeling emotionally and spiritually bankrupt – and ready to shop, partly because I needed to, but also just to numb everything since I was too tired to think. I bought whatever I wanted and arrived home that day with two store cards that I neither wanted nor needed. I'd said 'no' to store cards plenty of times because I knew that for me personally, the temptation to spend beyond my budget was too great. Too many gorgeous clothes to buy! This time I was too exhausted to think it through. As the saleswoman gave her spiel, all I could think of was how much easier it would be to give in today. Yes, give me everything! At least she would stop talking. In that moment I didn't have the capacity to think about why I'd said 'no' to store card for years. The bill that arrived the following month was a great reminder.

In the book *The Screwtape Letters*, chief devil Screwtape reminds Wormwood, his protégé, about how to exploit human weakness. 'Remember, he is not like you, a pure spirit. Never having been a human (oh that abominable advantage of the Enemy's!) you don't realise how enslaved they are to the pressure of the ordinary.'[7] What happens to you when you're enslaved to the pressure of the ordinary? Do you spend more, drink more, eat more? Do you become passive about the images that appear on your computer screen, or do you seek them out? Do you fall out with friends and family?

These things are all significant, but there is another cost. When Jesus pulls His disciples away from the hectic pace of life, it's generally a time of revelation. It's on retreat that Peter calls Jesus the Messiah (Mark 8), on retreat that the transfiguration takes place (Mark 9). In ordinary times of rest, switched off, hanging out in their community, they learn some remarkable things about Jesus that will shape the rest of their lives. Jesus wants to be with us in the ordinary, to speak to us, to reveal Himself to us. But when our lives are too busy, our heads too cluttered, we miss out because we miss Him.

AND SO, BACK IN THE REAL WORLD . . .

Do you see why rest is so spiritual? It's because life is! Life is spiritual. But back in the real world, it's hard. Taking a day off is challenging when you're raising a young family, looking after a relative and holding down a job! It's hard when you feel the pressure of work and responsibility. When Chris and I first married, our days off were spent with newspapers and lovely food, with long walks and seeing friends. Today we have young children and our jobs carry a lot more responsibility than they did in our halcyon newlywed days. So we find that we have to work constantly on this and find creative ways to set boundaries and rest as a family with kids who don't understand the concept of a lie-in! We try to make time to rest alone, and to rest as a family – with varied results!

Yet the challenge remains. To swim for our lives from a society that has no time to pause with wonder and recognise its Creator. To swim for our lives from a condition where loneliness and dissatisfaction, temptation and loss, can be buried under endless activity for weeks, months, even years. To swim from the idea that overwork is healthy and admirable. To swim from a cluttered world, and then to stop and deal with all that lies beneath. No, we can't cheat the Sabbath.

SO HOW CAN WE PRACTISE THE SABBATH?

- Work out how you rest – some people recharge alone, others recharge in other people's company.
- Choose the day – if you work on a Sunday (church, hospital, etc.), don't beat yourself up with guilt, just find another day!
- Look at your use of the computer/mobile phone – do you need them on?
- How can this day look different from the other days of the week?
- Do you need help to have some space? On our day off, we try to do something individual, and something with the four of us together.
- A whole day might feel impossible to begin with. Do you need to start with half a day?

- Do you need to look at why you overwork (at home/work/school, etc.)? What hides behind the activity – do you have something to prove, a fear?

Stopping and switching off gives me space with God, for God and with others. Do I have transfiguration-type experiences because we have a day off? Not really, but when I have a pattern of rest I notice that God's guidance seems to get through more easily. I'm free to enjoy the things offered by the life He has given me. I'm healthier in every way and more available to God, to hear Him, to receive Him, to be used by Him. It keeps me in emotional and physical shape for what's ahead.

Stop and take a long look at your life. Stop and engage with your life, with God's pattern. Both of these things help us withdraw from the pace of a society that is moving at breakneck speed. Both give us a chance to engage with God and the good things He has given us.

INTO THE TWENTY-FIRST-CENTURY DESERT

Yet the desert saints and many others through the ages who made similar choices were not just concerned about withdrawing from the world, living to a different rhythm. They deliberately chose to go into the wilderness to pursue God, to know Him, to hear Him. So now we've stopped and seen, and turned to a new direction . . . what could the desert look like for us in the twenty-first century?

I tend to live my life with a soundtrack. It's a soundtrack that isn't just music – it's sounds, activity, noises and movements that fill up my landscape. I'm a loud person, with a loud laugh; I enjoy noise and I love music loud. I thoroughly enjoy being busy and active and doing things. It doesn't agitate me, I actually find it energising, even soothing at times! It helps me concentrate. But even I know that there is such a thing as too much, and there's a time when we just need to get away.

There are times when we need to turn off the phone and the TV, put down the magazines and the books, quit the Tweeting, sign off Facebook and MySpace and lose the laptop – when we need to pull away from the frenetic pace of life, from an over-stimulated environment, and be *somewhere else*. Sometimes, in order to hear God clearly, to know Him, we need to get out of our environment and our everyday existence. It might seem impolite or antisocial to need space from people, but what it's actually about is creating a specific form of space for God. It's not about pulling away. It's about giving all that we have and are to turn towards Him. Sometimes the only way we can truly focus on Him is to simply get away from it all.

Throughout Scripture, there is a motif of God's people going into the desert and meeting Him with power, both individually and corporately.

TWENTY-FIRST-CENTURY DESERT COMMUNITY

When the saints retreated into the desert, many people followed them, forming desert communities seeking a new way of life. We too find power in taking time to retreat from the pace of life to pursue God together.

A few years ago I spoke at a women's retreat, hidden in the pine forests two hours north of Phoenix. The group spanned all ages, but there was a particularly large contingent of mums with young children present. It had taken a lot of organising to get there, but they had made it. As the retreat began, there was a giddy excitement in the air. At first glance it was like some huge pyjama party! The real picture is that a group of women who ranged from committed to overcommitted finally had some space and some time to meet with God and connect with one another. This weekend, they didn't have to look as if they had it all together; they didn't have to take care of everything and everyone. This weekend, they could talk uninterrupted to adults for as long as they wanted. They could eat meals that they hadn't cooked, and they could eat them warm. Yes, they were excited! The phones were turned off to wait for a more opportune time.

Many of these women were caught in the double bind of feeling that they needed to spend time with God, but when the day ended they rarely had the energy. At the end of the first talk, the group was encouraged to sit or lie down, to get relaxed. The lights were dimmed. For a brief time the room was silent. Then a woman read Scripture and prayed over the group with music in the background. A prayer team circled the group, pausing to pray silently over individuals and then moving on to someone else. It was quiet and simple and had a profound impact on everyone there. It wasn't every day that these women got to hear God's words to them, or have the space to receive them. It wasn't every day that someone took care of their needs. The retreat continued to be a powerful experience. They devoured the teaching, digesting it in groups, and prayed, sang, danced and lay prostrate in worship. Women met with God on solitary walks; they met with God as they listened to each other's stories of His love around a cabin fire. They rested, they slept, they laughed and they deepened friendships. And they were reminded that God knew their lives and considered them important. They returned home renewed and with a fresh revelation of God's character and power.

These women were a world away from their everyday environment, and it made all the difference. They didn't have to be alone to meet God. Indeed, many felt alone most days; they needed people. But they also needed a location where for a time they were away from everyday life. Away from life's necessities, they reconnected with the ultimate Necessity for everyday life.

Retreat can also take place in our everyday environment. My former church developed a pattern of prayer throughout the day. At fixed times during the day, church activity stopped as church staff, congregation members and members of the local community gathered in the sanctuary to pray. We'd enter the room in silence, leaving our conversations at the door. During the prayer time, sometimes we read liturgy, sometimes we listened to music. Most often we sat in silence. It was an opportunity to reconnect with God amid the business of the day.

Q. How can you retreat into the desert with your community? Can you get away with your church, your small group, your family?

ALONE IN THE DESERT

No matter who we are and what our personality type or stage of life, there is a time to be alone. Jesus retreated with His disciples, but He also 'often withdrew to lonely places and prayed'.[8] This was a regular pattern in His life. The desert saints retreated into isolation in order to draw closer to God. We too need space in the desert where we are alone with God.

Sandra, a wife and mother in her early fifties, had served God throughout her life. Her family played an active role in their church; she was committed and always volunteering in some capacity. Sandra was seeking something more and had always felt drawn to the idea of more contemplative forms of prayer, but she didn't know what to do about it. One day a guest speaker at the women's group led a quiet morning. It was a small group, and the quiet period itself lasted only ten minutes, but Sandra knew she was on to something. Next, she attended a quiet day which was a profoundly powerful time. It was just what she needed. There were no children to attend to, no shopping list to fulfil, just the chance to listen to God. In the following weeks and months, as well as attending quiet days, Sandra would be up in the night, alone with God. Eventually she started to carve out more space for times of silence and solitude. 'It was like a hunger to be there more often, to be where God was.' Alongside this hunger for God was a growing awareness of the Holy Spirit and His gifts. Sandra was not the type of woman who switched off easily, who would not be involved. But she was discovering that she needed to give God undivided time. For her, it was time to tune in to God in a new way.

Sandra's journey into silence and solitude was a gradual one over a number of years. It began with ten minutes, and then developed into a few hours. Later still it became a weekend. Over ten years since her discovery of silence and solitude began, her children have all left home, Sandra has greater flexibility and so might do five days or a week, or longer still. Some of us might wonder why anybody would want to do this. Others might envy her opportunity! At surface level it might sound as if Sandra was an active member of the church who opted out of life and hid away. What impact has 'the desert experience' had? Here's what Sandra has to say about it:

> There's something cleansing and purifying about being alone with God in silence. I can tell when I have not been away with God; I begin to see the warning signs in my character! Silence and solitude have opened me up to a deeper relationship with Him, a closer identification with Him. It's helped me sort out some unresolved areas of my life and been the context for God's healing. The Bible is more alive to me now, because when I am reading it I've got more of a listening ear. I'm tuning in to God and hearing things I was too busy to hear. It's helped having a spiritual director too, having someone more experienced in this to guide you.

As for her service, she commented:

> A lot of people asked me if I was opting out of the world. My experience has been that instead of being removed from the world, I come back more focused and more engaged. I hear more clearly, I see more. I have a deeper sense of compassion for people. Silence is to the heart what sleep is to the body. If we don't have it, we're in deficit.

DEALING WITH THE DEFICIT

'Silence is to the heart what sleep is to the body.' Are you in silence deficit? Do your heart and mind ever get the chance to be still? When we don't sleep we don't function well, and in certain situations (on the roads or handling machinery) we're dangerous. We've already seen that when we don't rest, we have nothing left to give to those who are important to us, and in our exhaustion we can make unhealthy decisions with significant consequences. What happens to us when we don't have silence? Have we missed God's words to us, God's healing, and His freedom? Have we missed God's compassionate heart for the world? Even when we fill our lives with Christian activity, songs to God, prayers to God, works for God, do we still have the potential to miss *knowing* God?

Perhaps there is a huge cost when we don't develop a pattern to be still. The problem we face is that silence is not easy to come by. What practices can we adopt to explore this aspect of knowing God?

We can create opportunities to retreat. We don't need to see retreats as just something we do in a specific place or time. We can retreat anywhere if we put our mind to it. As a single woman, I used to babysit a lot for families from church. As the children slept upstairs, I would make the most of the time and a different location to retreat with God and stop and listen. Are there opportunities you could create?

We can seize opportunities. I'm in a stage of life that doesn't seem to lend itself towards silence! I have two preschool-age children and my husband is a pastor. Our girls love early mornings! And like their mother, they love to talk and will continue to talk until they go to bed. But even the consummate extrovert needs to recharge. I've come to crave silence with God. Just to be with Him. Sometimes it's in the middle of the night: when one of the girls has stirred, I seize a chance for silent reflection. It's not because I'm especially spiritual, but more because having children seems to have played havoc with my body clock and I don't return to sleep easily! There is no one to take care of and nothing to do at that time, just me and Him. Are there everyday opportunities you can seize? For example, I do a lot of driving, so the stereo doesn't have to be on all the time.

We can start small. Sandra approached practising solitude and silence in stages. As she became more familiar with retreat, she extended the amount of time. Let's be realistic in our expectations as we try out a new practice. It might begin with a minute of silence, and over time progress to something more. No performing is required!

INSANITY

Albert Einstein described insanity as doing the same thing over and over again and expecting different results. I know I've been there countless times in my relationship with God! I've desperately wanted to see God move in my life, yet have held on tightly to pieces of the shipwreck. I've ignored what was happening in my life, the opportunities, the struggles, and the toll they took on my heart. I've clung to the values in society that felt comfortable to me, and crowded God out of my daily existence. Too cluttered to hear His voice, my faith was uncertain at best, and seemed irrelevant at times. Still, it took a long time before I thought about trying to approach things differently. Insane. Change will not come without changing. Is your life too cluttered for God to move near you, breathe on you and speak to you? If that is the case, explore the example of the desert saints and adapt those principles for your own life. Take a long, hard look at the world around you. Pull away from the pace and tone that is set by society. Pursue ways of reconnecting with God.

There is nothing more important than developing our relationship with God. So once we've begun to make room, what happens next? What can we do to establish a powerful connection with God? We'll explore some ideas in the next chapter.

8

Connecting with God

Let every detail in your lives – words, actions, whatever – be done in the name of the Master, Jesus, thanking God the Father every step of the way.
(Colossians 3:17 *The Message*)

The God, who speaks, speaks in the ordinary events and inter-actions of the day. What excitement this adds to a routine day!
(Ben Campbell Johnson)[1]

You talk to God, you're religious. God talks to you, you're psychotic.
(House, MD)

CONNECT AND COMMUNICATE

When we have taken an audit of our lives, we have an idea of where our hearts are at and the situations that excite, compel and concern us. As we pull away from the frenetic pace of the world around us, we have a chance to get rid of some of the clutter that fills our hearts. Finally there is some room to make a connection with God in a productive way. But how?

It's generally understood that good communication is an essential ingredient when it comes to developing and maintaining a healthy relationship. Communication is a vehicle to knowing someone and being known; it helps a relationship grow and mature. Marriage counsellor and author Gary Chapman suggests that there

129

are five 'love languages' of communication in relationships. He cites physical touch, acts of service, words of affirmation, quality time and gifts as ways of communicating love.[2] Whether we identify with his specific definitions or not, we know that, broadly speaking, there are many ways in which we communicate, shaped by personality and cultural preferences.

From the very beginning, God has sought a meaningful relationship with His people. It's a wonderful truth that, although we worship a God who is mighty and powerful, He has made a way that we can know Him personally and intimately. In order to respond to God's love and make a genuine connection with Him, we need to learn how best we can personally communicate with Him. For those of us who enjoy time alone, this has the potential to be the powerhouse of our faith. To the exuberant extroverts who spark off other people, this might feel like a prison at times, because they may prefer to connect with God as part of a wider community. If we are in a particularly demanding phase of life, raising a young family, caring for a relative, working extra-long hours, time alone seems inaccessible at best. When there is free time, choosing to be with God, though it seems as if it's what you *should* do, might be the very last thing you actually *want* to do.

There are a number of ways we can communicate with God. Prayer, worship, reading the Bible, fasting and silence are but a few examples. Our church traditions emphasise particular practices. Some would describe the devotional life as time spent with God (preferably in the morning, when we are alone with a Bible and a notebook). Others emphasise contemplative prayer. Some streams place a high value on engaging with the beauty of our environment, meeting God using all our senses. Others prefer austerity. Singing is optional, perhaps because it might feel a bit lonely on your own.

I grew up in a tradition that emphasised 'the quiet time', when you went into your room and read your Bible notes and prayed.

It has worked better at some stages of life than others. For years I tried to make God my first connection in the day. Then I tried establishing a quiet time with my preschool-age girls around. For a time I put on a DVD to distract them while 'Mummy talked to Jesus' and read her Bible. But they would always drift towards where I was sitting with the inevitable 'Mum, what are you doing? Can I join in too?' It was an endearing, sweet opportunity to explain to my girls how I talked with Jesus, but I still didn't get to talk to Him! I've needed to find creative ways to meet with God, and it's certainly taking time and effort to work on our relationship in this era!

Which one is the best way? Perhaps there is no best way, but a number of ways that will work. Because we are uniquely wired, we'll have different ways of connecting with God. We'll have different styles of prayer, different ways of worshipping, of reading the Bible. And with each season of life we'll find the need to make a transition and discover new ways and methods of developing our relationship with God. The point is not the practice, of course, but meeting God in it. Connecting with God in the reality of our lives is the non-negotiable element here.

My hope is that we'll find fresh life and renewed love for God as we look at different ways we can make a connection with Him.

MIX IT UP!

This chapter offers a few ideas that different people have tried for making the God connection. There are suggestions for prayer, reading the Bible, worship. Some may be familiar, so why not try ones that bring something new to your experience? Experiment with them; adapt them for your stage of life. Take note of which ones reflect well with your personality. Take note of the ones that don't – they might make a great fartlek someday!

Just try a few things. Variety brings something fresh to our relationship with God. We engage more, we concentrate a little more, which means we might not take communicating with Him for granted. It stops our spirituality from ending up in a rusty rut. If a practice doesn't work or fails to engage you, it doesn't make it bad, and it doesn't make you a failure. Put down your cultural 'oughts', ignore your ecclesiological 'shoulds', and see what else is out there.

PRACTISING THE GOD CONNECTION

Prayer – talking to God – is the most obvious practice we think of when we think of connecting with God. Throughout the Bible we see God's people lifting their voices in prayer, reaching out to God for freedom and deliverance, for blessing. As we look at Jesus' life, we see that prayer on His own, making the time to pray, was part of His natural way of being (Luke 5:16). We know from how He taught His disciples (learners) to pray (for example in Matthew 6:9–10) that prayer involved a level of closeness and intimacy (calling God *Abba*) and also an understanding of God's power and might (expecting a response: 'Your kingdom come').

Yet for us, sometimes this life-changing communication can feel so incredibly . . . dull. Guiltily and dutifully we carry on, hoping that God is not as bored as we are. We know prayer is important. We just wonder if everybody else has a prayer life that is more engaging and more effective than ours. Sometimes it's a matter of our expectations; not every prayer time needs to feel like a scintillating, life-changing conversation! Sometimes it's a matter of working on how we make the connection. We've already explored the role that silence and solitude can play in deepening our connection with God. But even things like *where* we connect with God can make a huge difference.

Sam was frustrated with the way he communicated with God. 'I go into my room, I shut the door. I sit in silence with my Bible and try to pray. It's awful, because I find it draining and I shouldn't.' Outside that tortuous half-hour, he was a creative, vibrant, outdoorsy type. He loved people and he loved life. Sam's friends suggested that perhaps he should use some of his God-given interests and abilities and offer them back to God in prayer and worship. Perhaps he could go hiking with God instead of attempting to stare meaningfully at a blank wall. They encouraged him to be creative with God, to play his instruments, to create his art, and take it from there. Sam got excited about spending time with God for the first time in ages and couldn't wait to get started.

In Exodus 31, God talks to Moses about Bezalel and Oholiab, artisans God had gifted to create the right environment for Him to meet His people.

> Then the LORD said to Moses, 'See, I have chosen Bezalel son of Uri, the son of Hur, of the tribe of Judah, and I have filled him with the Spirit of God, with wisdom, with understanding, with knowledge and with all kinds of skills – to make artistic designs for work in gold, silver and bronze, to cut and set stones, to work in wood, and to engage in all kinds of crafts. Moreover, I have appointed Oholiab son of Ahisamak, of the tribe of Dan, to help him.[3]

It's interesting to note in the creative context of this verse that we find one of the earliest biblical references to being filled with the Spirit of God. Centuries later, some of us find that environment and aesthetics play an integral part in how we connect with God meaningfully, both in corporate worship and on our own. Some people set aside a room, or space in a room, for prayer. While some like an austere environment, others want to make something more of where they connect with God, infusing it with colour, texture and fragrance. Still, a room doesn't work for everyone. Some people need to be among other people, even if they're not talking to them. So they need to go for coffee, or to a local park. My local Starbucks might as well be a church, for the amount of Bible studies, prayer times and God connections that take place over an espresso there. I once met a woman who said she liked to spend time with God sitting on the street (I guess on a bench!), because she likes company and there were always people passing by. She didn't talk to them, but their presence was enough. Some prefer long walks in the countryside, because the beauty of creation reminds them of their Creator. An urbanite friend likes to walk through the city centre, where he's reminded of the need to pray for his community. Churches and cathedrals connect us to the history of God's people through the ages, reminding us of a God who is present from age to age. Art galleries and installations can also be public places where we are reminded that God still seeks to communicate today in our world and culture.

Your environment matters.

Q. Do you have an ideal environment where you spend time with God? What makes it so ideal for you?

LIFE BEYOND THE QUIET TIME

Brother Lawrence (c. 1614–91) was a lay brother in a Carmelite monastery. Serving in the priory kitchen for most of his life, Brother Lawrence saw every moment, both mundane or profound, as an opportunity for deeper communion with God. His closeness with God was not slotted into a time frame; God was everything that mattered in Brother Lawrence's life.

> The most holy practice, the nearest to daily life, and the most essential for the spiritual life is the practice of the presence of

God, that is to find joy in his divine company and to make it a
habit of life.[4]

This brother's approach transformed not only his own ordinary
existence, but also the lives of the many people who sought him
out for wisdom and guidance, and the lives of those who continue
to seek out his insight through his written works. Brother Lawrence
illustrates a life with God beyond the quiet time, where God had
continual access to his heart and life.

The idea of a set 'quiet time' can sometimes limit our relationship with God to fixed (albeit regular) events rather than
allowing it to be a journey or pilgrimage. Our relationship with
God and the implications of His words do not end when the
event does. On a bad day it can have a 'let's get this over with'
feel, and for some it's simply just a bit too scheduled and planned.
Where's the creative spontaneity in a fixed time?

What could it look like to invite God into every moment of
our day, to worship God as we embrace menial tasks, to pray
continually? Ben and Helen, church leaders, offer a few examples
from their journey. This is what Helen says:

I've never liked the idea of a quiet time, generally because I am
not very good at it, so I end up frustrated! Over time, I've
learned to connect with God in my everyday moments,
communicating throughout the day, in every part of my life,
when I'm washing up, doing normal everyday activities. I do lots
of little things throughout the day. There's a hill I often walk up
when I'm doing errands. On my way out I pray about one
subject, my journey home is the opportunity for another. As a
result I find when I do have extended time it's so much better.
There is not the same pressure. It takes the pressure out of one
slot of the day that has to be my God time and so has to be
amazing. I also now find it easier to meet God in worship at a

church service because it's not all about the event at one time in the week. It's life throughout the week, and I've found it's much easier.

Ben, Helen's husband, is exploring something similar:

> Personally I have been trying to link events in the day with prayers. It reminds me that God is present . . . Walking into work, meetings, I link little events with a certain prayer. As a result I'm building up a routine and an understanding that God is present and close throughout the day. I've also found there's something of a rhythm to how I spend time with God, shaped by when our son wakes up! The rhythms and seasons of our lives change, so I'm drawn to practices that reflect and embrace that reality.

The church calendar can facilitate different ways of meeting with God throughout the year. Often rich in colour, symbol and liturgy, it's a great way to connect with our Christian spiritual heritage. Lent is one of the most well-known seasons, where culturally people give up things, because they know it's a good idea (or, if they are like me, seize another chance at a failed New Year's resolution). But liturgy can also take us on a powerful journey with God through everyday, ordinary life. Andrew, a thirty-something curate, notes:

> The seasons of the church year are important to me. The Collect prayer for each of the seasons is something that I can reflect on, day after day, for that season. For me, liturgy includes the arts, because it includes colour and symbol, things that speak to us at a deeper level than rational argument. In the Church of England, Advent and Lent are represented by purple; Christmas, Epiphany and Eastertide by white; days associated with saints

and martyrs (connecting us to our past) and with the Holy Spirit by red; and 'ordinary time' by green.

We might also have our own personal calendars which we work into our God connection. The New Year holds great personal significance for me, and Lent is a season with which I've always connected strongly. As I mentioned earlier, we've embraced the American festival of Thanksgiving as a season to recognise the wonderful things that God has done for us.

Q. How can you connect with God in the ordinary events of the day, week, month and year?

CREATIVE INTERACTION

Exodus 35 charts the story of God's people building a tabernacle, the place where they would meet with God. As you delve into the story, you see that the offerings God receives from the people are practical and tangible materials to build a meeting place that is interactive, sensory and rich in symbolism. Perhaps we could find ways of creative interaction today as we connect with God? Here is Helen again:

> When I am praying for something or someone specific I like to light a candle. It gives me something to focus on, and it physically articulates my prayer that God shines His light into the situation. When I've finished talking to God, I leave the candle lit, a constant reminder of my prayers, and the situation throughout the day.

Others love burning incense as they pray – as a reflection of the idea of the fragrance of Christ found in 2 Corinthians 2:14–15. The memories of our prayer life linger around our home far more than they would if we'd just prayed using words alone. Once a friend of mine led a group of tweenagers in a time of creative worship and prayer. They were given paints, textiles and clay and told, 'Now go and say what you want to God and listen to what He has to say to you.' At the end of the time a young boy showed me his 'quiet time'. It was a sculpture of a huge hand, with a person sitting in the centre of it. When I asked him to tell me about what he'd made, he responded, 'God told me that I am in His hands.' So simple and so powerful. I smiled as he walked away, profoundly affected by the way God had spoken to him. And to me.

A number of years ago, I came across Charlie Mackesy's work on the Prodigal Son and the Prodigal Daughter. 'The Prodigal Daughter' is a simple picture. A father carries his wearied, grown daughter in his arms, while she hides her face in his neck. It's hard to see if he's whispering to her, or simply holding her close. In the background you see the words of the Prodigal Son story as written in Luke 15. I bought postcards of the picture and gave them to some of the teenagers in my church. It blew them away, as each of them imagined themselves in the Father's arms. Scripture was communicated to them in a fresh way.

My friend Vanessa tells me that as a visual learner the use of the arts for Scripture ministers to her more than words ever could. 'You show me a picture of that story and I can tell you everything about it.'

SOAKING PRAYER

'So you put on a bit of music, lie down on the floor, and think of Jesus and call it *prayer*? You've got to be having a laugh! It just sounds like a cop out!' It might not have been what I said when someone first told me about the practice of soaking prayer, but I promise you, that was what I was thinking! Soaking prayer offers an opportunity to set aside space and time to be with God. Music is played in the background, sometimes with Bible verses read over it. The intention is to create a meditative and relaxing environment in which to rest and rely on God's love and strength, to listen to Him, to meet Him.

Ruth, a thirty-something missionary, found soaking a valuable expression of her prayer life.

> I put on some music, lie on the floor or curl up in a comfy chair with a blanket and then just rest. Sometimes I read the Bible, meditate on a passage, and ask God to speak into it. Other times I simply take my journal and let myself write. Sometimes during a soaking session, I find that God does bring insight into parts of my life. At other times, my mind wanders and sometimes I fall asleep! Yet after a few soaking sessions, I always feel more 'spiritually aware'. I find it easier to talk to God; I have a renewed passion for the Bible, or simply have a new perspective on my circumstances.

Ruth says she considers soaking a practical expression of King David's prayer in Psalm 139.

> Search me, God, and know my heart;
> test me and know my anxious thoughts.
> See if there is any offensive way in me,
> and lead me in the way everlasting.[5]

> Soaking gives me a chance to slow down and actually think about Him, maybe just a word, a verse, a theme. It's not about the music or the words of the music . . . it's just a way of getting 'space' . . . it starts a process that you then carry on through the day. When I'm going through rough times, it's

difficult to speak or read the Bible, but I know I need Him. Soaking is my way of saying to God, 'Here I am.' When I'm in a good place, it's just giving God time to have access to my heart. It's the opportunity for God to speak, to soften me, change, transform and fill me with His Holy Spirit. In the end I feel more in tune with God and able to give and minister out of love.

When you soak a dirty pan or stained clothing, the water and the washing powder get to work and lift the stains permanently. I've found that soaking prayer has done the same. Listening to Bible verses with no agenda, listening to worship music and just stopping, has given God a chance to get to work on my heart in the power of the Holy Spirit. His word gently scrubs at my bitterness, His presence soothes my wounds, stills my busyness. Maybe it's too easy; I don't do anything, I don't work hard at it. But then, did we ever? Jesus has always done it all. What could we add to the power of the cross? Maybe, like contemplative prayer, stillness before God is a very good response. And perhaps soaking prayer is a little easier for the extrovert types!

Prayer lists and journals can be helpful tools for people who like a more structured approach to prayer. I used to get frustrated when people would speak on prayer and say it's not meant to be a shopping list of requests. I love writing lists – how else am I going to keep track of what's going on? And I *am* shopping for answers. My own answers aren't working; I need help! I accept that these answers might not be the brand I want, or they might be delivered later than I feel I need. But when I've returned to a prayer diary months later and seen recorded the prayers that were so wonderfully answered, my faith is strengthened. A friend of mine, with a different approach, doesn't have a list of names – she slots photographs of people into her Bible.

CONNECTING WITH GOD'S WORD

> Every part of Scripture is God-breathed and useful one way or another – showing us truth, exposing our rebellion, correcting our mistakes, training us to live God's way. Through the Word we are put together and shaped up for the tasks God has for us.[6]

The Bible is amazing: a sixty-six-book library that God has given us, revealing His goodness, His greatness and His Word to us today. The Bible is integral to our spiritual growth and maturity. Yet there are many different ways to get into the Bible in depth. The Word of God has the potential to transform our lives, for ever. When we read the Bible, it's not just about information gathering; our aim is to meet God in His Word. But again we need to work out how we engage with His Word afresh so we don't miss out on all He wants to say to us.

Q. How can we delve into God's Word, soak it up, learn it, grow in it?

There are many tried and tested ways of getting into the Bible at a deeper level. Daily Bible reading notes are a great resource, helping us to shape our day with biblical insights, and are great when we don't have much time. But there are other practices that Christians have used through the ages that may help us dive into God's Word and connect with Him there.

A BIBLE LESSON FROM THE ANCIENTS

Lectio divina, Latin for 'holy reading', comes from the contemplative traditions of the Christian faith. *Lectio divina* is a spiritual practice which undertakes a prayerful, reflective reading of the Bible. Richard Foster describes it as 'the primary mode of reading the Bible for transformation', a practice concerned with depth of understanding rather than with how many chapters and verses of Scripture we read. 'Our goal is immersion,' he continues.[7] Though the practice varies in different traditions, *Lectio divina* leads us on a journey through reading, listening to God's promptings, and prayer and response.

In many ways, *Lectio divina* does not appeal on a surface level to my personality and way of doing things. Yet what I love about *Lectio divina* is that it's a practice that stops me from rushing through the text and it focuses my attention. It's a practice that draws me in, not into my own thoughts, but into the Bible, allowing the Word of God to speak to me. It gives me time to listen, to be encouraged and challenged. While other practices attend to my intellect, this practice creates room for the Bible to move among my thoughts and emotions, my hopes and fears. Scripture gets to work on me, leading to a prayerful response and an opportunity to rest in God.[8]

Another ancient tool, often used in *Lectio divina* (but also separately), was developed by Ignatius of Loyola, founder of the Jesuits. Ignatian meditation draws on the use of the imagination, so that after we read prayerfully through a passage of the Gospels, we dive into the passage as though we were actually there. We take in the sights, sounds and smells of the environment, employing all the senses. We then *imagine ourselves in the story*, perhaps as one of the characters. Ultimately, though, our focus is on *Jesus* in the story. We take in what He says to our character, digest His words, observe how it makes us feel, our response. The stories of the Gospels come alive in Ignatian meditation, leaping off the page into our daily lives. And, more importantly, it reminds us that our Saviour too is alive, walking with us in everyday life.

LOVING GOD WITH ALL YOUR MIND

'Christians should use and develop their mind,' writes Gene Edward Veith. 'The mental faculties of the human mind – the power to think, to discover, to wonder and imagine are precious gifts from God.'[9] We've already seen a few ideas exploring our creative capacity to connect with God, but there is more in our minds than our imagination. With our minds we interpret the world around us; we use our intellects to navigate our relationships and make life-shaping decisions. With our minds we process both the height of our joy and the depths of our suffering. Yet sometimes we fail to engage our minds to the same degree when it comes to our spirituality. We develop our minds at college and university in the light of our careers or personal interests, while our biblical understanding is weak in comparison. Maybe we're concerned that our intellects may act as a barrier to wholehearted devotion to God, or we simply don't see ourselves as the academic type. However, we need to train our minds to be spiritually fit for our journey with God. If we are not intentional about this, our minds are out of spiritual shape, left to be discipled by the lies of the evil one, our human condition and the values of a broken world.

We can use our capacity to think, interpret and process to go deeper in our relationship with God. We can employ our minds to watch our life and beliefs closely. Sometimes being stretched intellectually is an important part of that. Matt, a pastor based in the north of England, sees this as essential for our growth as Christians.

You are in charge of your spiritual diet, not your church leader. We need to take some responsibility for what we digest. Instead of just consuming all that is out there, make room for reflection in your life, so that you can process, test and apply all that there is to take from a given message.

When we think through our beliefs, it ensures that our faith is not just a passing fad or the product of what others have told us to believe.

One of the ways we can train our minds is through rigorous study. Disciples of Jesus are learners by definition, so we'll never need to stop learning! I've started taking theology classes at a local seminary. Here students are encouraged to treat study as a devotional practice, recognising that Jesus called His followers to love God with all their minds. My classes have provided a brilliant context to explore the Bible in a different way, a deeper way. I meet with God as I interact with Scripture. I am stretched in discussions with fellow students. We tackle theological ideas, and explore how these ideas intersect with today's culture. Our classes function as a think-tank, a support group, a challenge and an inspiration. Study has ignited my mind with a love and a passion for Jesus. I need to think and I need to think deeply, so why not think about Jesus? Some of us may be uncertain of where our God-given intellectual gifts fit in with our everyday faith; we're scientists, philosophers, futurists, culture watchers. Don't put your thinking to the side; instead find healthy, creative environments to love God with all your mind!

There are so many different ways we can take loving God with our minds to the next level. Have you tried any of the following?

- Memorise verses or chunks of Scripture.
- Teach the Bible – get involved in children's or youth work, or volunteer to lead your small group. Some of us find that we grow more by getting into God's Word in a community context.
- Blog about your Bible-reading experiences and interact with others.

- Maximise what's out there online, or use social media that help you connect with God.
- Read different translations of the Bible, for some variety.
- Use Bible commentaries, dictionaries and concordances as a springboard for your thinking.
- Read the works of some great Christian thinkers – C. S. Lewis, A. W. Tozer, Ravi Zacharias, to name but a few. There is so much out there!
- Read and research topics that you are passionate about; see what you can learn about them.
- Listen to it: use audio Bibles, listen on your iPod, MP3 player, in the car, at home.
- Create with it: take a passage in the Bible and paint, sculpt, collage, design, write a song or composition or poetry.
- Read devotional material written by Christians through the ages, from different cultures and communities.
- Try something without a plan or agenda!
- Contact your local theological college and see what is available.

BODY LANGUAGE

Therefore, I urge you, brothers and sisters, in view of God's mercy, to offer your bodies as a living sacrifice, holy and pleasing to God – this is your true worship.[10]

It's easy to internalise spirituality, making it an intellectual or emotional thing. But the Bible never made that distinction, and I believe we lose something when we do. Because every part of our life is spiritual, there is a physical dimension to our connection with God. It's found in the physical surrender that complete stillness requires. It's seen in getting down on our knees, lying on our faces before God. It's found in action songs and raising our hands, in singing, shouting, jumping and clapping as an offering to God. We see it as King David danced 'undignified' before God and all the people, as 2 Samuel 6 describes. I've known a number of dancers who found great freedom in their time alone with God by dancing, simply for Him. But I think there is more to it than that. It's as though our bodies are agreeing with or articulating what is happening on the inside. We love with all our heart, soul, mind and *strength*.

I've found that running has become an integral part of my spiritual life (and not just praying for survival). Some of that is enjoying the physical freedom that God has given me and sharing it with Him. On a practical level, I find it much easier to connect with God on the move. Life is active and hectic. I don't just want Him when I stop; I need Him as I move! I take a single verse with me to meditate on, or a topic to pray for. It's my thinking time, my place to surrender frustrations and work through confusion, to get out physically what I cannot say, and He's with me. Sometimes my run illustrates things happening in my own life in a way that sitting in a room never could. I run out of water and I'm thirsty and it reminds me of how much I need the presence and the power of God as I run my race. There is something *total* about it for me when my body is involved in prayer or Bible reading or worship (sung or otherwise). My voice is loud, but my body is louder.

Q. Does our body language communicate something to God?

Does what we do with our bodies say something to God? When unmarried Christians choose celibacy in a sexed-up world in spite of our God-given desires for marriage and intimacy, surely that says something to God? Something more than words – surely that is spiritual.

Fasting is another vital way in which we engage with God with our bodies. We deny ourselves in pursuit of Jesus. Most often it's food, for a period of time, a day, a few days. (Sometimes we fast from other things that play a big role in our lives – TV, computer games, retail shopping, mobile phones, social media such as Facebook, Twitter, etc.). It's not asceticism for the sake of it and it's certainly not trying to earn gold stars with God. In fasting we surrender our appetites and entitlements in an act of humbling ourselves before God. We see that in the Bible fasting was used in spiritual warfare, in resisting temptation, in acts of repentance, in seeking God's guidance. In *Experiential Worship* Bob Rognlien writes, 'Truly biblical spirituality is never divorced from our physicality, but always embraces the body as a sacred instrument of worship, designed to glorify God.'[11]

Q. What could it look like for you to offer your body as a living sacrifice?

BE INSPIRED!

There is incredible diversity out there for us when it comes to connecting with God. Try something! Try anything! Developing our relationship with God is the most important thing we could possibly do.

Depending on our stage of life, however, some of the ideas expressed in this book might still feel out of reach. A single mother may crave silence and solitude to be with God, but she's raising a family alone. When will she get the opportunity to connect with God in the way He's designed for her?

This is where community spirituality comes in. While some prefer spirituality in an individual sense, others are drawn to a more corporate expression of faith, a faith community. Yet a community spirituality is not just about worship services, prayer meetings and group Bible studies – valuable though they are. We see in the life of God's people that community was integral to spirituality. There was something spiritual in simply being together. It was a chance for God to meet His people, in tangible, accessible ways. We'll explore this in the next few chapters.

9

The life together – a glimpse of His glory

Human beings can't help it; we need to belong.
(Seth Godin)[1]

One of the greatest diseases is to be nobody to anybody.
(Mother Teresa)

Together you are the body of Christ. Each one of you is part of his body.
(1 Corinthians 12:27 CEV)

Somewhere on my journey I got it into my head that real Christian spirituality, real godliness, was to need no one but God. All I needed was my personal God connection. I was active in church life, doing church things because I knew those were important, but the corporate side of my spirituality began and ended in a Christian event or activity. I didn't understand what it mean to *be* the church. In my mind, Christian maturity meant being willing and able to depend on Him alone. It was as though the vulnerability of needing other people was a sign of weakness, lack of faith, or just a bit . . . fleshly! If I had a personal struggle, it was better to keep it to myself, unless it was a testimony *after* the event. Some of my thoughts were based on pride and fear. Some were simply that I was desperate to please God and tried hard to do the right thing. It's taken me some time to discover how integral our Christian relationships are to our spirituality.

RELATIONAL BY DESIGN

In the beginning, from the beginning, we were made for community. The opening chapters of Genesis show God creating and surveying all that has been made. The light was good. The seas were good, the plants and trees were good. The sun, moon and stars were good. The animals, fish and birds were good. There's only one thing that God said wasn't good: 'It is not good for man to be alone.'

It's astonishing that in a perfect world, something is missing. God is there; surely that is what Adam needs most of all? God doesn't think so. Adam needs to live in community.

Let that idea sink in. God is *not* enough?

We are relational by design, and so is our spirituality. God's values on relationship are displayed in His very being, the Trinity. Relational is not just what God does, it's who He is. Mal, a church leader who is passionate about the Christian life in community, puts it this way: 'The very essence of God is relational. It's God the Father, Son and Holy Spirit. So how can we talk about individualism, when the God that we worship *in His very nature* is *relationship?*'

This is the God who said, 'Let us make human beings in *our* image, in *our* likeness',[2] suggesting that we are designed to reflect God's relational values in our own relationships. Clearly God seeks out a relationship with each one of us, and we need to respond personally to Him. But to have a relationship with God while isolated from other believers overlooks a huge dimension of our design and our faith journey. Those of us who are introverted may not need as many people in our lives as extroverts, but everyone needs meaningful relationships. If we're looking for spirituality that works, we need to recognise the significance of relationships with other Christians. We belong together.

FRIENDS OF GOD

As Jesus walked the earth, embodying the life we're called to live, we see that relationships played a central role. Jesus spent all night in prayer about whom to choose to be in His core group of disciples. Mark's Gospel tells us, 'He appointed twelve – designating them apostles – *that they might be with him* and that he might send them out to preach.'[3] These relationships were not just about the phenomenal task ahead, nor purely so that *He* would be with them. It was so that *they* might be with *Him*. These were the main people Jesus chose to do life with. A closer examination of the Gospels suggests that Jesus appeared to have a smaller network in Peter, James and John, and then was particularly close to John, who was described as 'the disciple whom Jesus loved'.[4] Beyond the Twelve, we see friends like Martha, Mary and Lazarus, with whom Jesus also shared life. Jesus gathered a diverse community who probably would not naturally be found in one another's company. Why would anyone want to hang out with a tax collector, for example? They were seen as traitors and dishonest. Yet all these people's relationship with Jesus provided a context in which they would learn together, do life together. After only three years of life together with Jesus, the disciples had grown into a dynamic missionary community. Though they didn't know it, they were about to be released to change the world.

FOOTWASHING

So what does 'relational spirituality' actually look like? When we look at the Gospels, we discover that the disciples learned about Jesus together through teaching and discussions, and they learned how to do mission together when Jesus sent them out into the community. It's a picture that resonates with our experiences with other Christians in church or on mission trips. But the disciples would also discover that a key feature of knowing Jesus was to learn how to connect *with each other* in a meaningful, life-changing way.

John 13 tells the story of Jesus washing His disciples' feet before a Passover meal. In New Testament times it was customary to have your feet washed when you entered someone else's home, to wash away the dirt and effort of your journey through the city streets. It was a job considered so disgusting that Jewish slaves were allowed to refuse to do it. The task was reserved for those considered the least of the least – the Gentiles, women and children. If there was ever a time to say 'no' to foot washing, it was Passover weekend. The city was packed with even more people *and* their livestock! There was more dust and dirt, rotting food and animal filth lining the streets. More mess! So it must have been shocking to watch Jesus wrap a towel around His waist, get on His hands and knees and start washing His disciples' feet. He demonstrated that He was more than their Lord and teacher; He was now also their servant. One by one, He took hold of their dirty feet. He washed away the filth and the rotting food that had littered the city streets. He cleaned up the muck and the dust. He cleansed their cuts and grazes, tended to their wounds. It must have been uncomfortable for everyone, but for Peter it was unbearable: 'You're not going to wash my feet – ever!'[5]

Peter couldn't handle it. It doesn't seem right that Jesus, the Christ, should get on His knees and serve him with this unpleasant job. This man raised the dead and cast out demons! But perhaps there was more to it than that. Perhaps Peter didn't want Jesus to deal with *his* mess, *his* dirt, *his* shame. Jesus was his friend, his teacher, his Lord. Now Jesus was also the one who cleaned up his filthy mess. It was too much. When Jesus explained that Peter needed this, Peter finally relented. Then Jesus gave all the disciples the following instructions:

> Now that I, your Lord and Teacher, have washed your feet, you
> also should wash one another's feet. I have set you an example
> that you should do as I have done for you.[6]

The events of John 13 act as a powerful metaphor for Jesus'
followers today. We all have dirty feet. We can't help it; we pick
up stuff when we go through this life. The stresses and pressures
of work and relationships stick to us like dust on our feet. Sometimes
the journey takes an unexpected turn. Life goes wrong and we
end up covered in filth, someone else's or our own. Or life's road
is so tough for so long that our feet dry up, the skin on our heels
becomes cracked, leaving us exposed and hurting. At other times
we stumble on the road, and pick up wounds, cuts and grazes.
Sometimes the wound is so deep that we can only walk through
life with a limp. Jesus comes to wash our feet. His love and grace
gently cleanse and renew us; His power strengthens and restores
us. Sometimes it's hard to let Him do it; we'd rather He saw
perfect, unblemished feet, but we know we need the life He offers.
And there's a greater challenge. He calls us to wash one another's
feet, representing all that Jesus is to our fellow believers.

DIRTY FEET AND A GLIMPSE OF GLORY

It's hard enough to let Jesus in; but now He calls us to allow other
human beings in too? I don't want anyone to see my dirty feet,
let alone touch them. I want my fellow Christians to think that
my family life is perfect, that I'm successful in every way. I certainly
don't want anybody to associate me with any kind of filth. I don't
want people to see my wounds, or to discern my limp. I don't
want anyone to see me as I am, in case they judge me or, worse,
pity me. It doesn't seem safe enough; people might talk. It's simply
better if they don't see anything at all.

Yet Jesus calls us to do more than see; He calls us to help clean each other up. To refresh each other when we're weary, to wash each other when we're dirty, to help each other heal. I can understand why Peter initially pushed Jesus away. That kind of touch is terrifying. But it's the kind of touch that we so desperately need. We were designed to live like this, because in our relationships with other believers we catch a glimpse of His glory.

In biblical terms, 'glory' refers to the weightiness, the substance, the felt presence of God. Because we are *His body*, and not merely a human-shaped institution, God uses His Church as a context to express His love and faithfulness, to guide and lead us, to comfort and challenge us, to inspire us, to heal and liberate us, to bring security and confidence and, on occasion, to confront us. There, in our relationships with each other, we feel the substance of God and know His felt presence. God uses the Church, His body, to make who He is and what He does tangible and real. Have you seen this in your relationships with other Christians? Do you wash one another's feet and glimpse His glory?

THE LIFE TOGETHER

So how do we express this feature of our spirituality? We express it when the word 'church' is no longer limited to an event on Sunday, but embraces the reality of being the community of God on earth. No matter how wonderful our church events are, we'd all acknowledge that an hour or two a week is not enough to develop meaningful relationships with other Christians. Our lives need more time than that. Thankfully, church *is* so much more than an event, as the Christians of the New Testament illustrate:

That day about three thousand took him at his word, were baptised and were signed up. They committed themselves to the teaching of the apostles, the life together, the common meal, and the prayers.

Everyone around was in awe – all those wonders and signs done through the apostles! And all the believers lived in a wonderful harmony, holding everything in common. They sold whatever they owned and pooled their resources so that each person's need was met.

They followed a daily discipline of worship in the Temple followed by meals at home, every meal a celebration, exuberant and joyful, as they praised God. People in general liked what they saw. Every day their number grew as God added those who were saved.[7]

It's an inspiring picture of how God's people can be. The church was devoted to gathering for worship, teaching and prayer; they didn't walk away from that. Amazing miracles were taking place, the church was on fire! But we also read that the church continually devoted themselves to *the life together*, shared resources, meals together. They were intimately and intentionally interconnected and 'people in general liked what they saw' and joined in. The community in Acts don't just 'magically' get along. A closer reading of Scripture teaches that the early church grew through the trials, tests and triumphs of their shared life. There were conflicts, disagreements and challenges. But they were active and proactive in building and developing the life together in everyday life.

Q. Is church a place that you attend, or a community to which you belong?

THE POWER OF SOME

Is it possible to glimpse glory in everyday life? Absolutely!

The Church community has an enriching role to play in each other's lives. Our differences in age and stage, class and culture, do not have to keep us alienated from one another. In a highly individualistic Western world, the Church reveals that there is power in *some*. It's the power to dispel loneliness and alienation, to forge authentic relationships in a culture that is often too busy to make time for friendship. It's the power to live counterculturally when we share our resources. In sharing our money and our prized possessions, we tackle consumerist desires to acquire more possessions in order to impress or compete with our friends. It's just stuff. It's an opportunity to widen our networks of extended family, with people like us, and with those not like us at all. There we get past the masks we often present to each other, and allow ourselves to know and be known. There is the power to help someone become all that Christ intended them to be, and not just by teaching the Bible or praying with them, but through friendship and service. It might involve helping them with their responsibilities, giving an introverted mum a retreat day, or coaching a student in exam preparation. When I was single, I got bored of thinking about my marital status and envying other people. I decided to serve a church family instead. Mal and Chriscelle were good friends and had three young children at the time, so I offered to babysit on a regular basis. I'd turn up and there was a home-cooked meal and a family waiting to welcome me. It was great to experience family life (the fact that Chriscelle is an amazing cook helped tremendously) and see my friends get some much-needed time for themselves. For me, those nights developed into a monthly evening retreat with God. It was a mutual blessing.

The power of some has provided countless meals and so much more. People have paid for vacations or offered a place to stay. They've loaned, shared, even given cars. They have shared their resources. People with skills that I didn't have fixed things or gave me sound advice. There were friends who cleaned my house when our babies were born, provided meals, or just sat in the house for an hour so I could have a break, a shower and some time to breathe. The power of some has surrounded me in times of both celebration and crisis.

I've noticed two particular effects of the power of some. When I've doubted God's goodness, such expressions of love in my community remind me that He's a faithful provider who meets all my needs. And when I tell my friends outside church about the power of some, they are impressed or intrigued.

There is amazing potential in the life together, but where do we start? It was three years of doing everyday life before the disciples learned to wash one another's feet. We need to make room to get to know other Christians in the ordinary, regular practices of going to church together, being part of a small group, sharing resources and skills. It creates the opportunity to grow the kind of relationships where we can learn to wash each other's feet.

SOME SUGGESTIONS FOR 'THE LIFE TOGETHER'[8]

Our patterns of community life will inevitably differ according to our life stage and environment, so use these as a springboard for your own ideas. Do not underestimate the possibility of glimpsing glory in the ordinary things you do.

An idea for church: change where you sit at church. I know, it sounds radical. Go on, I dare you! That way, when you greet one another or share the peace, it's not just with other members of your family, or your best friend. Again. Choose to talk to someone new at church that day! Get plugged in to a social or ministry event at your church; put yourself in an environment where you'll meet some people at church. A silent prayer event is probably not the best one here, but you never know.

Get together with some people for a meal, or for some fun. Think of something you enjoy doing – going to a movie, having a DVD night at home, sport, a pub quiz, a book club – and invite people. Take the initiative!

How do you *express commitment to your community?* Commitment generally involves time, money and effort – sharing or sacrificing some of humanity's most precious commodities. Some of us are rich in time. Where could your time be spent in your community? Find someone in your community who is time-poor and see how you can help. If you're effort-wealthy, think of where you can invest your energies. Is there a practical need you have the skills to meet? Others are rich in money. Spend your money and bless those around you. I remember in my student days, when I had no money at all, I returned from class one day to find that two friends had bought me two weeks' worth of groceries. I cried.

Explore intentional community. This is where your community gathers around a specific vision. It might be a commitment to share life together at a deeper level, to take on a missionary project together, to share meals a number of nights a month, or to have people moving into your home. Whatever the vision is, it needs clearly agreed goals and a plan, which to the best of your knowledge articulates how you intend to reach those goals. Intentional community is expressed in a variety of ways, and may only be for a season. For me this has ranged from having a house night with my roommates when we ate together and checked up on how we were doing, through to emigrating to the USA with my community to serve at a church.

Q. Jesus had twelve people with whom He shared life. Who are the Christians with whom you share life? Are there new ways in which you can share the life together?

A GLIMPSE OF HIS GLORY: REDEMPTIVE RELATIONSHIPS

In community we not only get to be God's hands, we also get to express His heart. The Christian community opens the way for redemptive relationships, where God restores what we've lost or missed out on. It's the place where the lonely discover that they belong, the outsiders find a home, and the wounds we've walked with for years begin to heal.

I didn't understand what it meant to have God as a Father. The idea was distant information to me. I read many books on God being my Father; I went to many conferences and was prayed for and sobbed countless times. These things helped and got rid of a lot of pain. But I still didn't understand what fatherhood actually looked like, or what it felt like in everyday life. As a result I was still confused about how to relate to God. I learned it through figures in the church who became fathers by choice over the years. They gave me advice on topics ranging from career choices to cars. They made all the right noises when a potential suitor chose someone else. They challenged me and inspired me in equal measure. Years later, I *know* God the Father is not a hollow theological term, because people in my community revealed something of His attributes in the way they treated me. Yes, I glimpsed His glory and my hungry heart drank it in and became whole.

Debra has encountered freedom through her community:

As I've been more immersed in authentic relationships – I've experienced more healing than I thought I would ever see. I'd been sexually abused in childhood and then experienced different abuse in adulthood as I pursued my career. Though I'd moved on and been healed in many ways, there were still some things I've needed to resolve. It was members of my community who knew me and loved me that encouraged me to make an appointment at church to pray about my past. The prayer team included some of those from the group I do life with. They prayed into my history and the effect has been life-transforming. God didn't just heal my wounds; God took me back to before the wound and restored me to my original condition. Who would believe that that could happen? And it was my community who ministered to me through the whole process. It helps that they know me and walk through life with me. And the change in me is significant, and substantive.

Q. Has the church been a place where your broken relationships have been redeemed through new, life-giving relationships? Have you washed anybody's feet recently?

THE BODY NOT-SO-BEAUTIFUL

It sounds great, doesn't it, this glimpse of glory? Yet for many of us these experiences of church are fleeting, or sound like some utopian fantasy. Instead, 'being church' has been defined by boredom, loneliness, dysfunctional relationships, oppression, and men and women wearing so many masks pretending to be someone they're not that you'd think church was a masquerade ball. We're disappointed. Some of us encountered terrible things like Megan's story. Others walked away, not from God, but from church, because, frankly, the people in it were unbearable! They were selfish, judgmental, cliquey, too busy to notice us, because we weren't at the heart of the action, giving the big money or involved in the big projects. An hour-long event once a week was more than enough! In the light of our experiences, 'the life together' does not seem to have any spiritual value at all. However, we cannot get away from the fact that God *designed* us for community, and even goes so far as to call us His body.

Sometimes it's the infrastructure of church life, meetings and services that works against us building authentic relationships within the church community. There is no time, space or opportunity to meet and get to know people. When those things are available, then there's the infrastructure of our lives to deal with. We're busy people; it would require a lot to make room in an already crowded week to get to know people. When we were students living in halls, or living with roommates, when life was a bit more like the set of *Friends*, we were thrown together in community by circumstance and had time to spare. Developing a life together simply won't look like that now.

But sometimes the issue is internal. It's the infrastructure of our hearts that needs some work, because we'd rather not expose our wounds or vulnerability. We're jaded now. Have I been hurt by the church? Yes I have. I've felt betrayed, wounded, bitter, frustrated, and I've cried out to God for justice. Have I, part of Christ's own body the church, hurt another Christian? Most certainly, sometimes quite deeply. I've betrayed, wounded, left people bitter and frustrated and, perhaps worst of all, not even realised it. When I've discovered what I've done, I've cried out to God for mercy. I can be as much the problem as the solution. Cathy, a parish priest, puts it this way:

> Real Christian community is messy and you are going to get
> hurt. When people tell me their experiences of hurt in the
> church I have to tell them – 'And you'll get hurt here too, and I
> will disappoint you . . .' It's something we have to learn to

negotiate together. What Satan wants more than anything is for us to be isolated. What we have to figure out is how we remain connected to our community as we work through relational difficulties.

Then there's the vulnerability of simply being known. A footballer friend once said to me that when he and the lads played in the Christian league he saw a different side to them. 'For me, if you want to know the measure of a man, what his spirituality is really like, then you'll see his real character on the pitch,' he concluded.

Are we ready to be known, for people to know our gifts, strengths, weaknesses, habits? Are we ready to let people see life behind the mask? Cathy continues:

> There's a richness in journeying with people who know and see things that I really wish that they didn't. It's a more authentic relationship. Is it dangerous? Absolutely. There are reasons why we don't do this; it's hard, it's painful and it's messy. It's the cross.

Q. What are the wounds you still carry from relationships with other Christians? What do you need to do to move forward?

AT THE FOOT OF THE CROSS

The cross. The place where Christ's body was broken by pain unimaginable, yet also the place where God's redemptive power changed the world. When I think of the Church being Christ's body, I want to think of a body resurrected, resplendent, filled with life and light and power. Wouldn't that be amazing for us to be that as church, to reflect His glory as we go through our lives together? Yet the journey to that resurrection power is the cross, a place of nakedness and vulnerability, torture and pain, death to self. Maybe we need to recognise that the process of developing authentic relationships with other Christians will inevitably involve carrying our cross, denying ourselves daily and following Jesus.[9] It will involve laying down overcommitted lifestyles that leave no time for building relationships. It could mean the death of hiding our broken lives behind the verses we quote and the songs we sing. It could be the sacrifice of being vulnerable, as people discover who we truly are. The self-sufficiency to which we've become accustomed may have to be crucified. We may need to practise surrender in order to build authentic community. At some point we'll need to practise forgiveness too, if we haven't done so already. But it could also be a place to practise in pain, safely, until one day we can practise thanksgiving.

Still, the cross is not the end; it's the dawn of a new beginning, of the life together.

10

Sometimes you can't make it on your own

Two are better than one,
because they have a good return for their labour:
If they fall down,
they can help each other up.
But pity those who fall
and have no one to help them up!
(Ecclesiastes 4:9–10)

If you want to go fast, go alone. If you want to go far, go
together.
(African proverb)

SOUL SISTERS

In my first year at Sheffield University, I used to fast and pray for revival in the city. Never one to act with moderation, as my prayers became more fervent, so did the fasting. I couldn't help but notice I was also beginning to lose a few pounds. It made me feel . . . determined. To pray harder . . . or was it to fast more and lose more weight? Within a few weeks, I couldn't tell, and nor could I eat properly. I wanted to pray, but I *needed* to fast and it wasn't for Sheffield, or because I was a poor student (though I was!). I needed to fast because I wanted to slim down and get away from the body I was living in. I felt embarrassed and ashamed of myself, shallow and confused. Obviously I told no one.

I made friends with a woman called Emma from the Christian Union. We talked about how much we'd both appreciate someone to talk with and pray with about everyday stuff. We decided to meet and pray and have lunch. Later that week, as we prayed together, I knew I had to open up about my increasingly erratic eating habits. But because I was feeling especially gutless that day, I decided to pray it out loud in Emma's presence so she would know what was going on without me having to look her in the eye.

It's a bit awkward to pray about your eating issues and then have lunch. I pretended that everything was fine until Emma said, 'So tell me what's been going on . . .'

I talked and Emma listened. It was out in the open, my shame melted away and my confusion dissipated. At the end she said, 'Well, we'll talk about this for as long as we need to, and we'll pray. And then we'll have lunch.'

When Emma graduated and left Sheffield, Karen,* another friend from the Christian Union, and I decided to be accountable to one another about our lives and our walk with God. So for the next seven years we met virtually every Friday, from nine o'clock to twelve o'clock. We spent most of the time talking, but it wasn't shallow chit-chat. Our conversations processed the sermons we'd heard at church, the challenges we felt God was laying on our hearts. We talked about our dreams and our callings. We admitted the fears and insecurities that held us back. We shared our longings and broken hearts. We listened to each other and laughed, we let each other cry. Sometimes we challenged each other, called each other out on things in our character or actions that didn't reflect our faith. We confessed sin, we prayed for each other.

Jesus met with me in these accountable friendships. There He spoke to me, and moved in power.

Sometimes you can't make it on your own.

*Karen is not her real name.

THE PROBLEM WITH BIG CHURCH

For all that is wonderful about our church meetings, we know they are only one facet of the life together. Indeed, sometimes by their sheer size or style, church meetings can become an obstacle to meaningful relationships. The Sunday meeting is hardly ever the place where we get to know someone well; church is too big and we rarely have the time to talk to each other. In addition, the power of some can be intimidating. There are some topics that are too vulnerable, or simply inappropriate to share widely, even as widely as a small group.

So where do you go when you need to unpack how to apply the challenge of Sunday's talk to your marriage? How do you ensure that you follow through on the inspiring things that came up in your Bible study? Where do you turn when you sense God calling you to do something at work, but you simply don't know how? We need relationships with enough room and the time to process our journey with God in all our twists and turns, people who will help us watch our lives and beliefs closely. This chapter addresses two kinds of relationships in our lives that help with this: accountable friendships and mentoring. We'll look at accountable friendships first.

AN ACCOUNTABLE FRIENDSHIP IS . . .

We've already noted that Jesus was part of a wide community of people; He poured his life into twelve, shared significant events with three, and had one noted friendship within that group of three. Similarly, we see different types of friendships in our own lives. Some friendships revolve around an activity, like work or sport. Some are people we've grown up with, others are in our new small group. And some friends are closer than others, and there is potential in them all to be conduits of transformation in our relationship with God as we do the life together.

So why is a so-called 'accountable friendship' so important, when we are overcommitted as it is? Is this just another fad?

Our problem is that although we have great Christian friends, we don't always choose to be real with them, even as we walk through life together. We share our resources, but not our struggles. We admit our struggles, but neglect to mention our deep sense of shame. We're honest about temptation, but not so real about our sin. We wonder if we can be sure, really sure, that this is a safe place to talk and be heard. Alternatively, we're a bit concerned about our friend, a situation in their life, but say nothing. We don't like confrontation and besides, who are we to judge? So we stay silent. In contrast, an accountable friendship is one where you get a bowl of water and some towels, kneel down and wash your friend's feet. We see the filth and the dirt, we see the limp, and we don't walk away. We'll help our friend clean up, and encourage them not to walk down that path again. And then, when we've finished, we'll invite them to wash our feet too.

In everyday language, an accountable friendship is one where we give an honest account of what is happening in our lives, and we hold each other to account for the lives that we say we want to live as Christians. It's a friendship where we give one another permission to encourage, inspire, challenge and confront each other in our journey with God. In these friendships we take the bold step of talking about our temptations and weaknesses that have the potential to derail our relationship with God. We might discuss our alcohol consumption, an attraction/flirtation with someone who is not our spouse, our tempers, destructive thought patterns in our heads, our struggles in our faith. But it's not just a place for confession, it's a place of encouragement. We stand alongside each other as we respond to God's call on our lives.

We're the prayer back-up for each other when we share our faith at work, we remind each other of God's faithfulness and His promises. An accountable friendship is a confidential place, so it's a safe place; we know that our friend isn't going to spread rumours or, worse, the truth! It's a place of protection. One of the biggest weapons in our enemy's arsenal is shame. We stay trapped in patterns of behaviour, unable to share where we're at because, well, what will people think of us if they knew who we really are, what we've actually done? We've talked to God about our struggles many times, and hoped that would be enough. But it doesn't seem to address the shame or the struggle. Perhaps it's because sharing who we really are with others is often a major part of the battleground. We know that God knows our stuff, but the thought of anybody else knowing is something else. An accountable friendship is part of the breakthrough, tackling shame and fear as we safely share who we are, bringing it all into the light. It's a place of honesty, vulnerability and transparency. It's also a place of God's power.

We might find that many of our friendships have some of these qualities anyway; perhaps we've had accountable moments in times of crisis. An accountable friendship makes the commitment of meeting on a regular basis to talk and pray through the issues of everyday life, and in many cases addresses issues in our hearts before they become a crisis. And it's certainly not a fad, it's as old as the Bible. Take, for example, the story of David and Jonathan. David and Jonathan's friendship in the Bible gives us a classic example of an accountable friendship in practice. It wasn't an easy situation for either of them, as it became clear that King Saul, Jonathan's father, was jealous and tormented by David's presence. Then there was the not-so-small matter of Saul trying to kill David, to the point that David had to become a fugitive. It became a friendship that had to be honest and real. We see Jonathan's constant encouragement. Jonathan saw David's potential and God's call on his life, and he encouraged David, even though it would mean that he would forfeit his place as king.

> And Saul's son Jonathan went to David at Horesh and helped him find strength in God. 'Don't be afraid,' he said. 'My father Saul will not lay a hand on you. You will be king over Israel, and I will be second to you. Even my father Saul knows this.'[1]

Jonathan sought out David and 'helped him find strength in God'. Accountable friendships remind each other of God's plans and purposes, and hold us to it, even when we feel like giving up. They seek you out in the wilderness and remind you of God's greatness and help you back on your feet if necessary. I love the fact that the illustrations of accountable friendships here are of men: a giant-killer and a warrior prince, two seasoned military men getting real. Accountable friendships are not a gender thing; it's not about women deciding to share their feelings. This spiritual practice is a necessity for all believers.

The Celtic Christians of the early medieval period understood the need for accountable relationships as an integral aspect of their spirituality. Celtic spirituality strongly advocated the *anmchara*, or the 'soul friend'. The soul friend was the friendship of mutual trust and transparency and love, providing a context for mutual spiritual direction and mentoring. People would travel great distances to meet with a soul friend. So essential was the soul friend to the Celtic way of spiritual life that Saint Brigid of Kildare thought that anyone without a soul friend was like a body without a head.[2] Still, as romanticised as the phrase 'soul friend' sounds, these accountable friendships can be hard work, a spiritual discipline. It's humbling to admit my failures and weaknesses, my hurt and sin. It's raw being challenged by a friend with words that I know God has been trying to communicate and that I've been avoiding. But when I look back and think of ways the Lord has strengthened me or healed me, there's usually a 'soul friend' in there somewhere.

HOW TO DEVELOP ACCOUNTABLE FRIENDSHIPS

For some of us, the first step in developing accountable friendship is to step out of isolation and into Christian community, as explored in the previous chapter. But for most of us, we've probably all had accountable moments with our friends or prayer partners in the past, an honest conversation about an area of struggle. Sadly, though, all too easily we close up again, and hope that person has forgotten our moment of weakness. How do we develop accountable friendships?

We turn an accountable moment into an accountable lifestyle. On one level, we could just be more open about our lives when we meet with friends and ask for their advice and for prayer. But life often gets in the way, distractions abound, and our best intentions are buried by our nerves and fears. Though it feels more formal and structured, it makes more sense to set a regular time to meet with a good friend, knowing that your plan is to take the time to be accountable with each other and to pray together. Here are a few suggestions:

- Who would be a great person to be accountable with? Think about it, pray about it, then ask them.
- Consider how often you can meet, how long you want to meet for.
- Think about where you are going to meet. Going for a coffee/drink/meal sounds great in theory, but if all your friends visit the same places, will you be able to share what is happening in your life? In fact, do you want anyone listening in?

- Discuss together what your time is for, what you want to discuss. Are you meeting together to be accountable about a specific issue, or is it about life in general?
- Talk about how each of you handles challenge or confrontation. It'll help you learn the best way to communicate difficult things, and it reminds you that sometimes this is what an accountable friendship involves.
- Before the end of your time, pray for each other, listen to God on behalf of each other, find a relevant verse of Scripture.
- To hold one another accountable in areas of your life, you need to have a specific plan of action, so you can monitor how you're doing. Instead of saying, 'I've decided to spend more time with my kids,' try to be more specific. What are you going to do to make that happen? Follow up on your plan the next time you meet.
- Remember to celebrate the good things that are happening in each other's lives.

Accountable friendships can be life-transforming, but we can also benefit from support from someone outside our peer group. That's where a mentor comes in.

SOMEONE ELSE'S WISDOM

Mentoring is an integral part of our society, from the school gates to the boardroom. Our bookstores and magazines have many advisers, sharing their expertise. We go on training courses for work to improve our skills, to work better as a team, ultimately to bring our company success. Talk shows have unleashed a range of experts and life coaches giving counsel on how to get ourselves fixed. And then, taking it to a whole new level, we have reality TV.

No longer limited to daytime TV on obscure channels, prime-time TV shows teach us how to clean our house or how to cook. Some tell us how to dress; we learn how to lose weight and exercise. Others walk us through home improvements, or buying or selling a home. Some tell us how to be married or parent our children. We see the experts enter, and sometimes invade, a person's life on a mission to transform them. They watch their behaviour, practices, and so on, and critique them. They give encouragements and challenges, suggest a framework for change and guide them towards transformation and success. Often the mentor is quite blunt, willing to upset or anger the participant, for the sake of the ultimate goal. In an often emotional epilogue, a family or individual often thanks the mentor for coming into their life and being a catalyst for change:

'I don't know what we'd have done without you.'
'She's given me the tools to move forward from here.'
'I've found a new confidence.'
'My life has changed, for ever.'

It's a bit embarrassing at times, voyeuristic in some ways, yet utterly compelling. And in spite of the camerawork and editing, we still find nuggets of wisdom that perhaps might apply to our own lives, our own families. There's something significant in our culture's longing to learn, to be taught, guided, even led. Who was actually supposed to teach us these things we don't know any more? Society places high expectations on what we're to achieve in life, with few ideas on how to get there. Maybe we just don't know how to live any more. So we call on someone who knows more than we do to help us pay the price and learn the lessons to get the life we long to have. If learning from another's wisdom makes us healthier people, strengthens our relationships, makes us more effective at work, it's no bad thing.

'If you want to go fast, go alone. If you want to go far, go together.'

'IMITATE ME'

There's something true in this for our spirituality too. Someone who knows more than us can help us see where we need to be.

Paul's 'train yourself to be godly' statement to Timothy is found in the context of letters that mentored Timothy as both a church leader and a man. Paul met Timothy in his teens and then invested in him for many years as they preached the gospel and planted churches. Timothy needed Paul, he couldn't make it on his own. As they did life together, Timothy, an apparently self-conscious young leader, grew into one of the key figures of the New Testament church. But where would he have been without Paul?

In his conversation with the Corinthian church, Paul offers himself and Timothy as role models to follow:

> Therefore I urge you to imitate me. For this reason I have sent to you Timothy, my son whom I love, who is faithful in the Lord. He will remind you of my way of life in Christ Jesus, which agrees with what I teach everywhere in every church.[3]

Sometimes, you see, we just cannot make it on our own. Take the story of Esther.

GUIDED TO FULFIL HER DESTINY

King Xerxes was looking for a new wife and decided to try out all the available women in the region. Basically, all the women were taken from their homes and prepared for their night with the king. After that one night, they would remain in his harem, unable to return home or marry anyone else. But one woman was about to have her life changed for ever and become the queen of Persia. The king saw Esther, and utterly fell for her.

Though Esther was an orphan, she was not completely alone in the world. Her older cousin Mordecai looked out for her and guided her. Every day Mordecai went to the courtyard of the harem to find out how she was doing. He guided her and advised her through the process, advising her to keep her family background and nationality a secret. He could see things she couldn't; he knew of a greater and harsher world. Mordecai was Esther's support through bewildering times, and that support enabled her to navigate this unknown season of her life and bring some stability. Yet Mordecai was more than that – he would also become her challenger and confronter.

Haman, one of the king's advisers, hated the Jews and wanted to eliminate them and so tricked the king into issuing a law that endorsed the annihilation of the Jewish people. This was devastating. The community was in mourning and only one person could do anything: Esther. Mordecai sought Esther's help, but initially she was unwilling to get involved. She was preoccupied with her own situation. It was a risk to visit the king without his request, and he had not asked to see her for a month. Perhaps Esther was disappointed, feeling alienated. We can only speculate. But Esther couldn't think beyond her world. If there was ever an emergency to test her theory, the annihilation of her people was it.

At this point, Esther didn't need a hug and comfort as in times gone by; she needed a huge wake-up call, which Mordecai duly gave:

Don't think for a moment that because you're in the palace you will escape when all other Jews are killed. If you keep quiet at a time like this, deliverance and relief for the Jews will arise from some other place, but you and your relatives will die. Who knows if perhaps you were made queen for just such a time as this?[4]

Perhaps Mordecai was a little harsh; but alongside his blunt assessment of her actions were hints of her destiny. It was enough to make all the difference. Esther went from disappointment and resignation to risking her life to fulfil that destiny. As mentioned in a previous chapter, God is not mentioned once in the book of Esther – yet you see the hand of God all over Esther's life. You see His provision, protection, wisdom, challenge and call. And you see these primarily through the relationship she has with Mordecai. Mentoring is another glimpse of His glory.

WHY MENTORING IS SO IMPORTANT

A mentor has the potential to change a person's life, to be used by God to steer someone towards the Lord and their destiny. Our mentor's time and accessibility speak volumes about God's interest in every single part of our lives. A mentor can challenge us out of our apathy or sin, can comfort us, and can equip us to realise God's design for us in every part of our lives. Mentors can come in many shapes and sizes, guiding us in our relationships, our parenting, our friendships, career choices, workplace, and church-based ministry. And through them God whispers His wisdom.

PLEASE MAKE ME LAUGH AND TEACH ME

The year 1992 was the make-or-break time for my faith. I was eighteen years old and two years of feeling isolated as a Christian had eroded much of what I believed and what I'd once stood for so passionately. In an attempt to get my act together, I'd moved from life in central London to a Bible college in rural Derbyshire. The local bus service stopped at five p.m. I was surrounded by countryside and had animals in fields for neighbours. Furthermore, the college had a curfew on when I needed to go to bed – a rule begging to be broken, in my opinion. Everything was alien to me. I wondered if I'd made the right decision.

Carole was one of the staff evangelists, and I was drawn to her immediately. First, she was a black Londoner like me. I knew she'd know important stuff like where to buy quality hair products for Afro hair. Second, I wanted to know how she as a Londoner survived in such a different world. Finally, I was drawn to her incredible laugh. It was the laughter of a woman who was completely free, uninhibited. I had no idea what she was free from, but she was free. I knew that I wasn't, and I wanted to be. I hung around Carole like a bad smell, partly because I was hoping that some of that freedom would rub off on me. I sought her out to talk to, to listen to, and I constantly asked her questions. I have a pretty loud laugh of my own; it just wasn't free like hers. Perhaps I would have her laugh one day.

Over the next few years, Carole had a phenomenal impact on my life. She was wise, gentle, challenging, entertaining. Often she just laughed at me. Sometimes she just held my hand, even though I really wasn't into people doing that sort of thing, and she knew it. She pointed me to Jesus when I lost my focus. She reminded me of the love of the Father when I felt He loved everyone but me. She navigated me through my various forms of drama and melodrama. She wiped away snot and tears and tolerated hearing all kinds of language spewing from my mouth. She didn't indulge me if I had a pity party. If she ever got tired of talking to me, she clearly found someone else to vent to, because she never let me know. I badly needed what she had – freedom. And she was sufficiently humble and generous to share enough of her life with me so that I could learn from her. She handed out biblical truth and the tools to live by in a way that I just could not have received in a Bible study or a sermon.

Alf Waite was another staff evangelist and he was nothing like me at all. Alf hailed originally from North Lancashire, a farmer who met the Lord and wanted everyone to know about it. Quiet and self-assured, Alf was a guy who was always watching, always observing. He was full of quirky pearls of wisdom and practical advice and never afraid to tell you the truth. At the end of the academic year, the students went out on a three-week summer mission trip in teams. Teams were normally led by a staff member, accompanied by a second-year student. When Alf asked me to co-lead his mission team I was a first year and only nineteen. I was honoured, completely out of my depth, and the youngest member of the team. His mentoring through that trip in particular was a huge vote of confidence in me as a potential leader. I was encouraged to succeed and allowed to learn through failure. Alf's mentoring inspired me to get my life in order in places where I was dragging my feet. Someone saw me and acted on what God was doing in my life to give me an opportunity to explore a call. I'll be forever grateful.

DO YOU NEED A MENTOR?

Sometimes a mentor's role is to point you to Jesus in difficult times. They help you to process your thoughts and feelings, and they can also keep you accountable. Gabe, one of the young adults at our church, said this about mentoring:

> The biggest thing about being mentored was having someone who truly cared enough to roll up their sleeves and put their hands in my mess. He wasn't just trying to tell me what to do; he actually cared about how I was doing.

Sometimes a mentor's role is practical and specific. As we seek to walk with God in our everyday life, we're left asking many practical questions. How do I parent my kids? How do I deal with ethical issues at work? What's the best way to handle money? Do I really want to marry this person? Obviously we'll seek God's guidance in prayer and in the Bible, but sometimes we'll find answers through the advice and experiences of people who are further along in life than we are.

Mentoring can last for a fixed period of time or can be an indefinite arrangement. In what area of life would you appreciate a mentor? If mentoring is something you'd value, why not talk to your church leaders to see if there are any mentoring opportunities available in your church community?

COULD YOU BE A MENTOR?

My husband Chris says:

> What I love about mentoring is that you help people see and engage with what God wants to do in their lives. And on top of that God uses you to change lives. The lessons I've learned on my faith journey are now used to help someone else on theirs.

Most of us don't see ourselves as mentors before we're asked, so perhaps we've never considered it, but perhaps we should. There are life experiences, stories with God, skills and talents that we could share and invest; we could encourage and equip someone else in what God has called them to do. So what do you have to offer?

- Some friends of mine encouraged their children to choose new godparents as they approached adolescence. Their

children chose young adults whom they admired and respected in the church family, who would mentor them and help them navigate their faith through their teens.
- Maybe you could share some of your thoughts and experiences on marriage with engaged couples?
- Perhaps there are people in your congregation who are entering your profession. What could you offer them?
- Perhaps you've met someone who has just become a Christian and is trying to work out what their new faith will mean for their old life. What could you share with them?

Some Christians have been walking with God for thirty, forty, fifty years, with faith that is fresh and alive.

Since my youth, God, you have taught me,
and to this day I declare your marvellous deeds.

Even when I am old and grey,
do not forsake me, my God,
till I declare your power to the next generation,
your mighty acts to all who are to come.[5]

Q. Could you be a mentor? Why not talk to your church leader about how you could serve in this way in your church family?

TIME-CRUNCHED? HOW ABOUT MENTORING A GROUP?

You may not have the time to mentor all the young professionals seeking your input. How about mentoring them as a group? It's not a new idea. John Wesley organised Christians into class meetings for mentoring and accountability – guided by a list of searching questions about their personal lives. During my time at St Thomas's in Sheffield, we adopted something of this model, calling them 'Huddles'. The staff team of men and women met with Mike for an hour every week. This wasn't a business meeting; this was a chance to talk about life. A list of questions was the springboard to our discussions. They revolved around the following points:

- *Our relationship with God*, with questions like 'Do I make enough space for prayer?' or 'Am I obedient to God's promptings?'
- *Our relationship with others*, such as 'Is my family happy?' and 'How are my relationships with my friends?'
- *Our relationship with the world*, like 'Am I proud of the gospel or ashamed?' or 'Do I leave time for relationships with non-Christians?'[6]

Each person picked a question that seemed to connect to their situation and shared why it seemed relevant. Mike and the rest of the group would offer reflections, insights, sometimes more questions. It was a great way to be mentored, because we learned from each other as well as from Mike, who led our Huddle. It also gave us the confidence to mentor other groups of people.

RELATIONSHIPS THAT LEAVE A LEGACY

God transforms our lives through . . . people. We don't need to try to make it on our own. If we can get past the inhibitions and pretences in our friendships, if we can get close enough to see and speak into each other's lives, we'll wash one another's feet and catch a glimpse of His glory. God takes stories of our lives with Him and uses them to bless and equip others. If we can drown the voice of our own inadequacy and offer what we have, we'll help others begin to realise their God-given potential. A phone call, an email, grabbing a coffee, doing lunch – they can all go a long way. They can all offer another glimpse of His glory.

John Wesley's last letter was written to William Wilberforce, a British politician greatly influenced by Wesley's ministry. Wilberforce faced huge opposition in his fight to see slavery abolished. Wesley's letter included the following words:

> Unless God has raised you up for this very thing, you will be worn out by the opposition of men and devils. But if God is before you, who can be against you? Are all of them together stronger than God? O be not weary of well doing! Go on, in the name of God and in the power of his might, till even American slavery (the vilest that ever saw the sun) shall vanish away before it.

History reveals that Wilberforce continued the fight against slavery for the rest of his life, until the battle was won. Relationships make a difference; they even help change the world.

11

A walk across the park

The worst sin toward our fellow creatures is not to hate them, but to be indifferent to them: that's the essence of inhumanity.
(George Bernard Shaw, *The Devil's Disciple*, Act II)

Any religion that professes to be concerned with the souls of men and is not concerned with the slums that damn them, the economic conditions that strangle them and the social conditions that cripple them is a dry-as-dust religion. Such a religion is the kind Marxists like to see — an opiate of the people.
(Revd Dr Martin Luther King)[1]

You are the salt of the earth . . . You are the light of the world.
(Matthew 5:13–14)

HISTORY-MAKER

I don't usually cry over a film, but this time, as the credits rolled, so did my tears. I simply couldn't help myself; I was overwhelmed by feelings of awe, gratitude, challenge and conviction. I'd never been so inspired. I'd been watching *Amazing Grace*, the film that tells the political story of the fight to end the slave trade in eighteenth-century Britain. The film resonated with me on so many levels. What struck me most was the relentless tenacity of William Wilberforce and his fellow abolitionists. To use the words from John Wesley's final letter, quoted at the end of the previous chapter, they were *not weary of well doing*. In the face of huge opposition, they fought for decades against the incomprehensible evil of slavery. 'God has set before me two great objects,' said Wilberforce, 'the suppression of the slave trade and the reformation of manners' (by which he meant morals in society). With this in mind, Wilberforce was a lifelong campaigner on many issues, including prison reform and education. This was spirituality in action.

'Maybe we can change the world,' I thought as I left the cinema. Maybe the songs we sang at university prayer meetings about history-making and serving the purpose of God in our generation still had something to say. It might look different from what I'd expected, and it would most probably take much longer than I'd imagined, but changing the world *is* God's agenda. It always has been.

As followers (instead of fans) of Jesus, we're seeking to imitate the pattern of life that He illustrated for us as He walked the earth. We see that His life had a dimension that stayed connected to the Father. We see His expression of 'the life together' with others. But we also understand that He lived, taught, demonstrated and shared the good news with the world around Him. As imitators of Christ, we need to take a closer look at this aspect of our spirituality. We'll explore this in our closing chapters, looking at how spirituality means that we communicate God's love to the world around us in both our words and our deeds.

GOD SO LOVED THE WORLD

God's intention was always that humanity would have a close relationship with Him, living under the benefits and the boundaries of His rule and reign. Yet in a single moment, humanity chose to step away from their relationship with God, seeking life on their own terms, with staggering consequences. It was a choice that would be echoed in the lives of men and women throughout human history, again with huge consequences. Many of the pages of global history tell the stories of human greed and selfishness, the shed blood of the innocent, poverty and loss that could have been avoided and, on particular pages, the reign of unspeakable evil. The world was ruled by values and activities very different from those that God had intended and desired. Still, Eden was not the end of God's role in human history.

We see God's intervention in history when He delivered the Israelites from slavery in Egypt, when He rescued His people from Haman's grasp in the book of Esther. We hear His heart and His concerns for the state of the world when He raises up prophets like Zechariah, Isaiah and Amos to speak His thoughts on injustice in society. And though these words speak directly into a specific context, they present a timeless challenge for God's people:

> This is what the LORD Almighty said: 'Administer true justice;
> show mercy and compassion to one another. Do not oppress
> the widow or the fatherless, the foreigner or the poor. Do not
> plot evil against each other.'[2]

He informs His people, then and now, that His concerns are their concerns too:

> Is not this the kind of fasting I have chosen:
> to loose the chains of injustice
> and untie the cords of the yoke,
> to set the oppressed free
> and break every yoke?
> Is it not to share your food with the hungry
> and to provide the poor wanderer with shelter –
> when you see the naked, to clothe them,
> and not to turn away from your own flesh and blood?[3]

God also reminds us that we can't simply hide away in our worship gatherings, oblivious to how we behave and respond to the world around us:

> Away with the noise of your songs!
> I will not listen to the music of your harps.
> But let justice roll on like a river,
> righteousness like a never-failing stream![4]

God so loved the world that He couldn't stand on the sidelines of history any longer. He got personally involved. Jesus left the glory of heaven and came to earth, proclaiming and demonstrating God's mission for humanity. He stood in the synagogue and explained the manifesto of the kingdom:

> The Spirit of the Lord is on me,
> because he has anointed me
> to proclaim good news to the poor.
> He has sent me to proclaim freedom for the prisoners
> and recovery of sight for the blind,
> to set the oppressed free,
> to proclaim the year of the Lord's favour.[5]

He taught values concerning life, love, money, power and relationships that were not the values of human kings or emperors, but the framework of life in God's kingdom. His teachings were radical and relevant then, and are radical and relevant now. His actions challenged the bigotry and injustice that lay entrenched in the culture. When Jesus healed the lepers, they were freed from the pain of isolation for being 'unclean' and were restored to their community. Jesus treated women differently from what was generally considered acceptable in that society. He even spent time with hated foreigners. He dined with outcasts and sinners, with the morally reprehensible, the dirty, the unclean. And in the face of a society that considered them worthless (even the religious rulers), He *loved* them. He confronted the spiritual powers of darkness and set captives free. He communicated the good news of the kingdom of God with His words, His deeds and His love in action, His death and resurrection. And He commissioned His followers to continue His work.

> Therefore go and make disciples of all nations, baptising them in the name of the Father and of the Son and of the Holy Spirit, and teaching them to obey everything I have commanded you.[6]

Throughout history, Christians have responded to His commission. They've followed in His footsteps, speaking out, demonstrating the values of God's kingdom in various ways. They've dared to stand against the cultural tide and fight for a better way, for God's way, and they've seen God change the world. Wilberforce was one of many. John Wesley's ministry had such an impact that historian Elie Halevy cites Methodism as the reason why England did not descend into revolution like France or other European countries. We've seen it in the civil rights movement with Revd Dr Martin Luther King in the USA in the 1960s. We saw it in the Christian opponents of apartheid like Archbishop Desmond Tutu, whose voice rang out along the corridors of power in the 1980s like an Old Testament prophet before an apostate king:

> Let me warn the government again. You are not God. You may be powerful, but you are mortal. Beware when you take on the church of God. Emperor Nero, Hitler, Amin, and many others have tried it and ended ignominiously. Get rid of apartheid . . .[7]

Many Christians have reached out to the poor and needy, mirroring the tender compassion of Jesus. Mother Teresa's ministry in Calcutta was an obvious example. Many people, like Jackie Pullinger in Hong Kong and Heidi and Rolland Baker of Iris Ministries in Mozambique, meet practical needs, but also emphasise sharing the gospel and ministering in the power of the Holy Spirit. And alongside these are countless other names worldwide, names known only to God Himself. They are praying, advocating, campaigning, serving, preaching, ministering in the name of Jesus to the lost, the least, the broken and the forgotten in response to God's call.

When I think of these history-makers, I feel proud to be a Christian! They are so inspirational, I feel honoured to be part of such an incredible family. But I also feel intimidated. From the outside looking in, these Christians are spiritual giants with more boldness, more love and more compassion than I seem to possess. I don't think I could ever do what they do. But a closer look at Scripture teaches us that taking part in God's mission is not just something we do. It's part of who we are.

SALT AND LIGHT: MADE TO BE MISSIONAL

'You are the salt of the earth . . . You are the light of the world,' says Jesus, communicating something of His disciples' identity.[8] What did He mean?

I have a friend called Martin who is a pioneer missionary, involved in projects in England and Rwanda. His passion for the gospel is infectious, and I've always admired his confidence. He's always involved in something which seeks to see every area of people's lives transformed by the gospel.

Yet Martin wouldn't say he's the most confident person; he feels nervous and uncomfortable just like everyone else. But he realised that engaging in mission wasn't so much about finding the right topic or technique, but about understanding and agreeing with his God-given identity. 'Jesus said you *are* the salt of the earth, you *are* the light of the world, and *then* outlined what that looked like in practice. Sometimes we just don't believe we are who God says we are.'

Do we believe that we are who God says we are? We are the salt *of the earth*, the light *of the world*. Jesus describes an aspect of our spirituality that is active and engaged; both salt and light are interacting with the world. Our spirituality is part of something far bigger than individual lives. Still, for either salt or light to make any difference, they can't be locked away. Salt is pointless until it's out of the container – it needs to be shaken and sprinkled or rubbed in. A lamp is simply ornamental until it's switched on in the dark.

John Stott unpacks the challenge of what it means for us to live in the reality of our spiritual identity:

Our Christian habit is to bewail the world's deteriorating standards with an air of rather self-righteous dismay. We criticise its violence, dishonesty, immorality, disregard for human life, and materialistic greed. 'The world is going down the drain,' we say with a shrug. But whose fault is it? Who is to blame?

Let me put it like this. If the house is dark when nightfall comes, there is no sense in blaming the house, for that is what happens when the sun goes down. The question to ask is 'Where is the light?' If the meat goes bad and becomes inedible, there is no sense blaming the meat, for that is what happens when bacteria are left alone to breed. The question to ask is 'Where is the salt?'

Just so, if society deteriorates and its standards decline, till it becomes like a dark night or stinking fish, there is no sense in blaming society, for that is what happens when fallen men and women are left to themselves, and human selfishness is unchecked. The question to ask is 'Where is the church? Why are the salt and light of Jesus Christ not permeating and changing our society?'[9]

For some of us, to see ourselves as salt and light in the world is particularly powerful. Because while we know prayer is important, and we tolerate going to church, it's outside the church's walls that our faith comes alive! It even frustrates us that the church doesn't spend a lot more time engaged with the outside world. Another friend of mine, named Kim, a committed Christian, described her faith journey this way:

> Even though I was in a wonderful church, I felt like I was missing something. I felt we'd individualised salvation, and missed so much of what true spirituality was. The heart of God is missional; so his mission couldn't just be an 'add on' to spirituality, something we do from time to time. It *is* spirituality. I realised that there was more to the cross than just me, there had to be something far bigger than me in all of this. It was about the Body of Christ *out there in the world*.

Spirituality is active, regardless of who we are. In the same way that we are designed to draw near to God in close relationship, to share the life together with other believers, we are designed to impact and influence the world, in the name of Jesus, extending the kingdom of God on earth. And as with the other aspects of our spirituality, we need to engage with it as we seek to imitate Jesus.

GET YOUR HANDS DIRTY

A number of years ago, the student congregation I led held a barbeque in the park on a hot summer's day. The aim was simply to have fun together. However, when we arrived, the park was filthy. It was littered with rotting food, discarded beer cans, broken bottles. The bins had overflowed and under some trees lay dog filth and used needles. Initially, we looked around and located a nice part of the park to have our barbeque time. But we couldn't take our eyes off the state of the park. There were young families there, with kids trying to play amid the mess. I turned to one of the team and asked, 'Do you think we need to do something about this?'

'Exactly what I was thinking,' was the response.

We bought loads of bin-liners and gloves and got to work, until the park was completely transformed. Some of the students bought treats and gave them out to whoever was in the park. Our fellow sun-worshippers couldn't get their heads around why we'd do such a thing and asked if we were a community service project! We formed little teams and spread out around the park, making the most of lots of opportunities to talk with people about Jesus.

I felt quite noble. Weren't we amazing? My passionate student congregation was out there talking about Jesus and people were being touched. I was – I mean, *it* was – wonderful. After basking in my synthetic glory for a few minutes, I decided to talk to some people and sat down to make some new friends. I wasn't watching where I sat, but noticed my hand felt rather warm and something didn't smell good. I looked down to see that my hand was in dog filth. And I thought I heard God say, 'Joannah, it's time to get your hands dirty.'

Though I wish it hadn't been communicated quite so *tangibly*, it was a challenge that I needed to hear, and still need to hear. All too easily, I like to put myself in the nice clean part of the park, where it's neat and clean and I can enjoy my wonderful Christian community. I get great teaching, amazing times of worship and rich relationships with Christian friends. What more do I need? In the meantime, the world's overflowing with need, and a feature of my relationship with God lies dormant, because it comes alive on the *other* side of the park. But on the other side it's messy, time-consuming, risky, dirty. Sometimes, if I'm honest, I simply don't care enough about life outside my immediate world.

I see harrowing pictures in the news of a desperate situation some-where in the world, a grave injustice, and my heart is broken, but only for a moment, until a familiar TV show soothes my shock and restores me to apathy. Jesus' life presents me with a constant challenge to engage my heart and get my hands dirty.

Q. Is it time to get our hands dirty?

A WALK ON THE OTHER SIDE OF THE PARK

If the church has been our sanctuary, our place of healing and freedom, it can be a challenge to even want to leave it. It's far better than the darkness and decay we've left behind. That nice, clean part of the park is great for us and for our families: why would we be anywhere else? For others it's the thought that our lives are already full enough. Amid our many other commitments it seems that there is no time, no room in our hearts and lives for yet another thing, another cause. Nonetheless, if we don't find ways to engage with the world that exists outside our church doors, then it's almost as though our church communities are flooded, blinded with light, while an entire stratum of society struggles around in darkness. Our church communities overflow with more salt than we'll ever need, and with gifts and abilities that are under-utilised while our culture decays.

It's hard to engage remotely; on the safe side of the park the world is far away, and because we're not close enough to see things clearly, perhaps it doesn't seem so bad. We think to ourselves that maybe people will see the light from a distance and come our way, be drawn to us somehow. They know where they need to go for salt. They know what we think.

Still, in the midst of our busy lives, Jesus says that salt and light is who we already are, and not solely what we do. As Jesus' followers, we need to find ways to reflect our God-given identity and walk in His footsteps. How do we re-engage and reconnect with our God-given commission? How can we be salt and light, interacting with, affecting and changing the world, with our very different personalities and gifts and life stages? It will look different for each of us in practice, but engagement generally involves investing our time, money, efforts and resources on the other side of the park.

Here are a few suggestions of habits to develop to help you re-engage.

Time

- Take the time to watch or read the news.
- Take the time to learn more about who lives in your city and community.
- Take the time to pray about how Jesus wants you to walk in His way as a lifestyle.
- Find out what is happening in the world through organisations like Oxfam or Tearfund.

Money

- Sponsor a missionary.
- Sponsor a child in the developing world. It's an incredible investment and a privilege to be involved in changing the world. See www.compassioninternational.com.
- Give to a cause you believe in, locally, nationally, internationally – just because.
- Give to established missionary organisations and development agencies.
- Consider what you spend your money on.

Effort and resources

- What skills do you have that could benefit others?
- Walk/drive around your local community and observe its needs. How can your observations inform your prayer life and your actions?
- Participate with mission activities in your church.
- Serve in a local homeless shelter.
- Visit a needy area in your city or region.
- Commit to doing a mission trip.
- Recycle.
- Reuse – donate your gently used clothes and possessions to good causes.

Q. What other ideas can you think of?

Perhaps we all need to take a stroll on the other side of the park and engage with the world as Jesus did. Instead of a one-off event that leaves us feeling noble, it could be a habit that we cultivate. We can develop spiritual disciplines of active engagement to follow in His footsteps towards a broken world. There we'll smell the stench of decay, and it might just shake us up enough to be salt. Perhaps when we tread in something, we'll realise that the world around us is not well lit and it will switch us on. There's a range of ways in which we can walk through the park; there's lots to do out there. There's no need to feel envious or inadequate about what other people are doing; the broken bottles need to be picked up just as much as the used needles do. Some of us will find ourselves serving in the far-flung corners of the park. Others will find that where we end up is actually our local neighbourhood or workplace. The key issue is that we all, in some way, follow in His footsteps in how we relate to the world around us. Jesus left the splendour and majesty of heaven to engage with a broken world in every way. As His followers, we're called to do the same.

Below are just a few practices that illustrate how we can be salt and light in our life with God. They are by no means exhaustive; they barely scratch the surface of the need in our world. Use them as a springboard for your own ideas; try them alone or with your friends. And remember that spirituality is practical; consider what habits you want to practise as an expression of your relationship with God.

SALT AND LIGHT IN ACTION

Salt brings a distinctive flavour to a meal; you know when it's there. Jesus' followers are distinctive; their presence permeates their surroundings. What could it mean to be the salt of the earth in our local community? It could mean that we are neighbours who look out for other members of the community, particularly those who live alone. We could take responsibility for Neighbourhood Watch programmes, or take an interest in local amenities and services. We could be the household that is known to be friendly and accessible. I've known some Christians make a point of baking cakes when someone new moves into the neighbourhood, as a way of introducing themselves. They're certainly remembered, and it's a great way to build relationships. In a world that is often too busy to stop and make friends, we can redefine what community life looks like, restoring meaning to community relationships.

Consider how you could be the salt of the earth in your community, and consider what you could do – if some of your Christian community or your small group worked together.

What would it mean to be the salt of the earth at work?

Would you arrive at a different time, talk in a different way? What would people know you for? Would you be a confidant, the unofficial chaplain of the department? Would your ethical values enhance your work colleagues and the company? Has God given you opportunities for wider influence through your job? Perhaps it seems obvious, but when we remember how God used biblical heroes like Joseph and Daniel to make a difference at work, we can see the potential in the impact we can make in the ordinary, obvious areas of life. Emma, who works for the NHS, says:

> I think it's also about going the extra mile for people, doing the mundane stuff that people don't really want to do and doing it with a joyful attitude. It's also about being consistent in your display of character and being aware that you constantly influence those around you. At work I pray a lot for my friends around me, their situations and families, but also I am aware that I carry God's peace into that place and His Presence.

Not only is salt a flavour-enhancer, it's also a powerful preservative, an antiseptic that prevents decay and corruption. Because we're the salt of the earth, following in His footsteps means we don't passively shrug our shoulders as we watch the world go by. Surely we address those decaying values where people are mistreated on account of their skin colour, nationality, gender, age or sexuality. To be salt of the earth means that apathy is not the inevitable response to corrupt practices within our workplace, or in the world at large. It may mean we engage with retailers and corporations if we discover that their practices damage the well-being of other human beings, even if those same practices appear to benefit us. It means we seek to walk away from that indifference to human selfishness and greed, even our own. Salt is an enhancer, but as an antiseptic it may sting. We might not always be popular for our stance on issues.

Q. What issues do you see that need salt to stop society from going rotten with selfishness and greed? How could you address the issues you see?

On dangerous icy roads, salt is an essential part of the grit spread so that we can travel safely. What does it mean for the Jesus follower to be the grit that enables people to walk through life safely? Perhaps it means that we invest our energies and resources in those who are vulnerable in society, the voiceless, the disadvantaged?

This is how Zoë, a stay-at-home mum, responds:

> As a full-time mum, I can often feel like I'm just not out there, 'engaging in mission' as many people would call it. But I've found this to be untrue. Since becoming a mother, my heart hurts so much more for children in need, both in my community and overseas. As a result I've chosen to make it my 'mission' wherever I'm at in life to engage somehow in some small way to make a difference.
>
> I choose to do something. I commit to the children in the developing world by sponsoring them throughout their childhood years. I choose to make it a priority that I will continue to extend our small family here in the UK by welcoming in children (albeit at long distance) and although my hands can't physically reach them in Tanzania or Brazil, I feel blessed enough to support them financially, in prayer and by encouraging words through letters I send, to give something to them and ultimately show God's love.
>
> As for the children I see every day in our community, that's harder for me. In this case I choose to pray for the people I come across and try not to judge. I also give to a local church who make it their 'mission' to put children's and youth ministry at the top of their outreach and praying that this will build up the resources of the youth and children's workers who work with

the local children day to day, those who are building relationships with these kids hoping that through this mission, bit by bit, lives may be touched and reached by the love of Jesus.

How could you respond? Could it be any of the following?

- To explore the services in your local community crying out for volunteers.
- To mentor a troubled teenager who needs help and support to get through school.
- To serve the refugees in your community as they go through the lonely and often bewildering experience of adapting to a new culture.
- A more permanent response, such as to foster or adopt children.

What could it mean to be the light of the world? Light illuminates a pathway, gives direction and exposes the darkness. Jesus followers illuminate, show up things for what they are, even when it's uncomfortable. One such 'illuminator' I know is a friend called Ben Sanders, a minister in Phoenix. Whenever I get an email from him, I feel a little nervous, because I know I am about to be challenged on every level. Ben has lived in Phoenix all his life and knows the city well. He knows what's happening in local government, and he knows the needs of the city. He knows about the people we've all been too busy to remember, and he reminds us not only that they are on God's heart, but also that they are a priority. Sometimes I wonder if it's a bit like listening to a twenty-first-century version of Amos, the shepherd with the serious reality check for God's people. So Ben's emails, blog posts and conversations call his brothers and sisters to prayer and action, they remind us of what the Bible says about justice (he tells me there are three thousand relevant verses), they remind us to turn up to key meetings, to reach out to the growing refugee community in Phoenix, to remember the poor, and also to remember those in power who decide their future.

Q. Do you engage with local politics or government policy? Where is your voice heard on behalf of the poor and needy in your community? What would it mean for you to act as light in the world?

These are mere examples and, as I've already mentioned, we've barely scratched the surface on ways to live as salt and light in our world. Our efforts may not seem as 'significant' as the Christian heroes we referred to at the start of this chapter. Our attempts to recycle and reuse may not be seen as being as 'spiritual' as serving overseas in Mozambique. Our signed petitions and letters written do not seem as 'influential' as addressing in person those who walk the corridors of power. History, however, may tell a different story, but even that is not the point. The reason we take our place on history's pages is because of the One who went before us and turned the world upside down. We've learned from Him that God loved the world so much that He got involved, sending His Son to redeem a broken humanity. Jesus' actions demonstrate God's heart.

We are walking across to the other side of the park because that's where Jesus would be, where He's always been. We serve because it's a good thing to do, but also because it's the God thing to do. We get the amazing privilege to be partners in God's mission – to be salt in this earth, to be light in this world. We get to be the defenders of the defenceless as we communicate what people are truly worth and point society to a healthier and fairer way to live. We may not be the best at it (just as we might not be the greatest prayer warrior), we might feel self-conscious and awkward, even afraid. Yet in spite of how we might feel, we're demonstrating the values of God's kingdom. When we walk across the park, we become His hands and feet. We get the chance to show God's amazing love in action, to people who may never have known or experienced His love and compassion. And alongside sharing His love and compassion, we also get to share His story – the story of a Saviour, a story that saves lives.

12

Lifesaver

*But you will receive power when the Holy Spirit comes on you;
and you will be my witnesses in Jerusalem, and in all Judea
and Samaria, and to the ends of the earth.*
(Acts 1:8)

Q. Do you remember who first introduced you to Jesus?

On Sunday 15 May 1983, my elder brother and I were taken to
visit the church on the high street, Springfield Methodist Church
in South London. It stood in the heart of an urban landscape that
seemed to stretch for miles, as one council estate ran into another.
In the decades to come the community would embark on the
process of regeneration. But this was the 1980s. These were the
days of urban decay, of a broken community and a simmering
'melting pot' which would from time to time erupt into racial
tensions, culture clashes and a few miles away the occasional riot.
Springfield was a church that had seen better days – more vibrant,
congregation-filled days. Instead of using the auditorium at the
back of the building, the congregation now used the modest
chapel at the side. We were introduced to a couple named Margaret
and Maurice Morton, lay workers who oversaw the youth and
children's work at the church. A warm and friendly couple, they
invited us to all the activities on offer for our age groups. For me
it was 'Junior Club' on Monday nights, and Fish, the children's
Bible study group on Friday evenings.

I turned up to Junior Club, a night of games, table football, table tennis – the usual 1980s fare, but with a God slot at the end. There were lots of kids there because it was a safe, fun place to be for children in the community. I knew so many of them. We were the kids from the council estate; we came from families that ranged from together, to broken, to 'interesting', to dysfunctional, to dangerous. Some of us were from families that practised other faiths.

On the surface, Margaret and Maurice might not have seemed the obvious choice as inner-city youth workers. They didn't appear culturally relevant, or streetwise. The music playing was dated, the games were not the best or the newest. And yet Margaret and Maurice were perfect, because our greatest need was to know all there was to know about God. And they poured their lives into us so that we might know Him. They were fun, and silly at times. They gave us time, and they talked with us and listened to us.

At the end of our Monday night games would come the 'epilogue', a fifteen-minute God slot. Every week we'd learn something about Jesus and how you could get to know Him. I'd heard of Jesus, I'd prayed before. But this was different. They talked as if they knew Him; they spoke of Him as though He was right there with us, and as though it was the most natural thing in the world for me to know Him too. It didn't matter that I was only nine years old; in their eyes I was old enough to be taken seriously. The more I heard, the more I wanted to know. Every week I turned up with questions about Jesus and what He was like, and every week they did their best to answer anything I asked and give me books to read. One July night that summer, I sat in my bed, did my best official prayer and gave God my life. And in case it didn't work, I encouraged Margaret and Maurice to do an altar call at Junior Club so that I could do it more publicly.

Margaret and Maurice didn't just inform me of a decision I needed to make about Jesus, they introduced me to a life with

Him. I learned a lot at Fish, the children's Bible study group. It didn't matter that we were children or teenagers; they shared everything they knew, often as they were learning it themselves. We raised money for missionaries and for the persecuted Church around the world. We learned about fasting, spiritual warfare, prayer and reading the Bible. We learned about the power of the Holy Spirit, His gifts and fruit, then prayed to be filled with the Holy Spirit. We learned how to talk about Jesus with our friends and share all that we had received from Him. We saw people healed, lives changed.

Though we saw amazing things happen over the years in the youth and children's ministry, the Mortons experienced huge amounts of hostility and criticism from much of the wider congregation. They had a small group of friends who supported them, but others who just thought they were wacky, too serious, and disagreed with their approach. In my teen years Margaret and Maurice knew their work was done, and they moved to a cottage in the Oxfordshire countryside. Though misunderstood on earth, my guess is that heaven will reveal their true legacy.

Who introduced you to Jesus? Is there a huge Christian heritage in your family? Or was there a friend in your life who had something different about them, and the difference was Him? Maybe it was an Alpha course, or someone handed you a Bible. Maybe Jesus introduced Himself to you in a dream or vision. However you first met Him, there was some form of introduction and it changed your life for ever. Wouldn't it be amazing if God could use you to change a life, to save a life?

Jesus demonstrated the good news of the kingdom in His actions, through a ministry of miracles, teaching, love and compassion, but ultimately in His death on the cross and His resurrection. Now we have peace with God, forgiveness, healing, salvation, freedom! This is still good news, and it not only changed the world, but the course of human history. We already know that

Christian spirituality is outward-focused, reaching into a hurting, broken world. Yet we're not only His hands and feet, we're His vocal chords too. His heart's desire is that everyone would know Him and be saved (2 Peter 3:9), and we have good news to share.

So who are we talking to?

FRUITFUL SPIRITUALITY

Maybe we've decided that talking about Jesus is not our thing. It's not one of our passions, and it's certainly not one of our gifts. If the need arises we'll acknowledge our faith happily, we're just not that intentional about sharing it. It doesn't come naturally to us, as we think it might for an evangelist or a priest. Or perhaps we're so immersed in our Christian community that we actually don't have any meaningful relationships with people who don't know Jesus. We are happy to serve, to get our hands dirty, but please don't ask us to say anything! I believe that if we stay in that mindset, we're missing out on something significant. Our spirituality is meant to be fruitful.

Often our first thoughts on being fruitful as a Christian lead us to Galatians 5:22–3, where Paul talks of the fruit of the Spirit. And rightly so, because following Jesus does have an effect on our character. His character is reproduced in us – and that's the fruit. Still, there is more to fruit than character. On the night before He died, Jesus described His relationship with His disciples as a vine and branches. Jesus was the vine, the source of life and sustenance, and the disciples were the branches. He told them that as they remained connected to Him, they would be fruitful.

> You did not choose me, but I chose you and appointed you *so that you might go and bear fruit* – fruit that will last – and so that whatever you ask in my name the Father will give you.[1]

'That you might go and bear fruit' is an active phrase. Fruit does refer to Christ-like character, but it also refers to people, the people who come to know Jesus through our lives and our words. The effect of our close relationship with Jesus is that as we imitate Him we share the good news as He did. As a result, other people come to know Him. Even in this Jesus has gone ahead of us, He's already appointed us. Fruitfulness is not just for the Christian professionals, for the special evangelists; we all get to join the fun. Fruitfulness is part of our spirituality.

ONE BEGGAR TO ANOTHER

Sometimes the biggest challenge to sharing Jesus is not external, but internal. Even with the tools, events and ideas, it can be scary sharing Jesus with people. We know that not every response is going to be a positive one. We fear rejection, mockery and embarrassment. We don't want our relationships or career progress to be adversely affected. And frankly, we like to be liked. Jesus doesn't promise us an easy ride, either. He described His disciples as 'sheep amongst wolves' or, worse, 'lambs amongst wolves'. Neither image conjures up a sense of reassurance in terms of our personal safety. It sounds as if we're about to be torn to pieces and devoured!

Yet, as Scripture tells us, God's power is made perfect in our weakness.[2] We cannot save anyone; we cannot heal anyone; we cannot change anyone. And we rarely, if ever, feel competent (or even confident) about sharing Jesus with people. Yet because God's in it, lives are changed for ever through ordinary people like you and me. Evangelist D. T. Niles said that it's 'one beggar telling another where to find bread'. It's an awesome privilege to be invited to share the most important news humanity needs to hear! We're just not that sure how to do it . . . However, there are some principles we see displayed in the life of Jesus that we can take up for ourselves as spiritual practices for our life with God.

LOOK FOR A PERSON OF PEACE

In the Gospels (Matthew 10; Luke 10), Jesus sent His disciples out in twos as mission teams to the surrounding villages. He gave them specific instructions about where to go to. Jesus told them not to get distracted by the people who were not interested in the message, but to focus on the person of peace:

> When you enter a house, first say, 'Peace to this house.' If a man of peace is there, your peace will rest on him; if not, it will return to you. Stay in that house, eating and drinking whatever they give you, for the worker deserves his wages. Do not move around from house to house.[3]

A closer look at these passages shows that Jesus described a person of peace as someone who:

- welcomed them;
- listened to them;
- served or supported them.[4]

There are people in our lives who are not interested in the gospel at all. In fact, they might even be hostile. And that's OK – we don't need to harass them with the gospel, or feel rejected. We can keep on praying for them, praying that they are bombarded with the love of God in a range of ways, praying for the time when they're ready to hear about Jesus. But there are others, if we were to take a closer look, who are people of peace. They like us, they listen to us, they even serve us, look out for us. They could be people we've known for years, or people we meet fleetingly. The main thing is that they're people of peace; that's where we start.

Jesus sent the disciples out in teams. Who is your team? Are the members of your small group reaching out together to reach your people of peace? Is there an accountable friend encouraging you and praying for greater boldness?

Who are the people of peace in your life? At work? In the football league? Your neighbour? Whoever they are, here are a few ideas to consider.

LIVE THE LIFE

This is not so much an idea for a habit to take up occasionally, but a principle for our lives. We need to live not as fans of Jesus, but as followers.

When I was sixteen, I started at a new sixth form college to study my A-levels. After years of being a closet Christian, I decided that things would be different from now on. Still coming down from that spiritual lift of a Spring Harvest conference, I made plans to save everyone in sight. I wore a huge wooden cross, a fish brooch and Christian t-shirts. I wanted people to ask me about what I was wearing. I told people I was going to church and invited them along. I wrote songs and poems and gave them to my friends to read – they were basically tracts telling them to become Christians. I seized opportunities to share my faith, whether people wanted to hear or not.

By the end of the year, my friends were long gone and I was incredibly lonely. I felt like a fool; it hadn't worked. People didn't ask what I was wearing; they asked *what on earth* I was wearing. People had tired of me, and so had I. One day, thinking long and hard about it, I came up with the idea that I could make it better.

If I just toned it down, maybe if I was more like them, had a drink now and then, had some fun now and then like they did, maybe they'd see that Christians had fun too. And maybe they'd like me – I mean like Him – again.

So I started over as a new woman. I worked hard to change. I stopped talking about Jesus, I stopped living for Him. I drank like my friends, spoke like my friends, flirted like my friends, lived like my friends. Completely transformed, I won all my old friends back. At the end of the year I was hanging out in the pub with the friend I'd missed the most. Smiling warmly, he turned to me and said, 'Jo, when I first met you, you were really holy. And now? Well, now you're just like one of us.' He was right; my hard work had paid off. The saddest thing is that I took it as a compliment.

Is that just the story of a teenager wanting acceptance, or does it ring true elsewhere in life – in a club on a Saturday night, at a dinner party with sophisticated company, with a crowd in the office, or with the other mums at the park? When was the last time you deliberately went incognito as a Christian, so much so that there was no evidence that there was anything different about you?

Jesus offers His followers 'real and eternal life, more and better life than they ever dreamed of'.[5] Do people see a life worth having in our lives? Remember the people who led you to Jesus – wasn't there something about them? Something in the way they lived their life, the way they spoke. Did they have a peace about them that just didn't add up, a security? Did they have a story that blew your mind?

You see, our lives talk. Our healed hearts talk. Our healthy approach to relationships talks, our ethics talk. Our language talks, every single thing about us talks. What do our lives say? Jesus was amazingly good news to the people around Him. Are we? As my friend Martin says, 'We're supposed to be a walking, talking spillover of heaven!'

Q. Do you live like a fan or a follower?

CAN I GET A WITNESS? SHARE YOUR STORY

Do we need to talk about our relationship with God more? It sounds obvious, but it bears repeating. We might have assumed that people aren't interested in Christianity. Though people may not be interested in the God they've heard of or the Christian religion they've seen described in the news, they might still be interested in Jesus, the life-transforming Saviour you know. I've often had to remind myself that there's no need to be ashamed of the gospel. As Paul writes, it's the power of salvation for those who believe.[6] Why act as though Jesus is my secret Sunday friend?

So now I make a habit of sharing what God is up to in my life with my friends. If God has provided a financial miracle, I tell them. When God has helped me, I tell them. I've invited them to join us on social justice projects we support. When He saved Zoë's life, I told them. If there's something I've found in the Bible that day that really helped me as a mum or a wife or something, I tell them. Sometimes people are excited for me; sometimes there are awkward silences (don't you just *love* those?), or things that people dismiss. But that's OK, we're still friends.

When work colleagues talk about what they did at the weekend, why does getting drunk have to sound like the most impressive thing out there to do? You might have seen someone healed, heard the testimony of a marriage restored, or been involved in some incredible project in the community serving the poor. Seriously, it's worth sharing and much more interesting! You don't have to be melodramatic about it – simply tell your story.

Q. What's your most recent story of God at work in your life? Have you told your person of peace about it?

TALK ABOUT JESUS

Our testimonies are honest accounts of a real God in real life. They often counter some of the images of Christianity that are in people's heads. They indicate that Jesus is real and relevant. Still, it's important that we work out how to explain who Jesus is, and what He has done for us in simple terms. Language like redemption and atonement, even the word 'sin', may be meaningless to some of our people of peace. So what will we say? We also need to be sure that we are not trying to be so persuasive that we water down the power of the message. Ronan, a missionary and teacher, found that he needed to pay attention to what he communicated about Jesus:

> Previously, when I used to share my faith, I used to talk about a God-shaped hole in a person's heart. But I found that with the people I spoke to, it gave the impression that the gospel was more about self-help or therapy: 'come to Jesus to make your life better'. Later on, when that person went through a crisis, they felt short-changed. What happened to this Jesus who made your life feel better? Now, when I talk about the gospel, I prefer to focus more on what Jesus did on the cross. I think it's huge that people hear about the cross because it's seen as nice but irrelevant.

How would you describe the gospel message?

In his letter to the Christian communities scattered through Asia Minor, Peter advises:

> Always be prepared to give an answer to everyone who asks you to give the reason for the hope that you have. But do this with gentleness and respect.[7]

Sometimes in our conversations with people, lots of questions arise. (I find this happens a lot with the people of peace I meet on a plane or on a train journey.) There are questions about suffering, or science, or philosophy. Some questions are asked out of intellectual curiosity. Some, particularly those on human suffering, may have a more sensitive personal backdrop. Some of our people of peace are currently committed to other religions. Processing someone's questions can be a huge part of their faith journey. Are we prepared?

Obviously we can't be good or knowledgable about every topic on earth, and we certainly can't predict all the questions people will ask. However, God has given the body of Christ some incredible thinkers who have dug deep into these subjects for us, and through books, talks, websites and training days can help us to be prepared. It's easy to avoid this and assume that it's simply not the way we share our faith. Instead, let's view this as an opportunity to get our minds in shape evangelistically as we prepare to share the gospel.

Here are some ways you can practise to be prepared.

- Imagine what you would say to your people of peace about Jesus if you're asked. Write it out if you find it helpful. Practise sharing the gospel message on your own, or with a group of Christian friends. It may sound contrived, but practice helps you communicate what you want to share more clearly.
- What are some of the Big Questions you've been asked by non-Christian friends? Find some appropriate resources to chew on. See if your friend wants a copy. Read it too and see what it brings up next.

- Read some Christian thinkers – Saint Augustine, C. S. Lewis.
- Read or listen to the works of Christian apologists – the website www.theocca.org might be a useful place to start.

LET YOUR LOVE BE LOUD!

As we've already explored in the previous chapter, love communicates too. It's especially true of people who see us day in, day out, like family members and long-term friends. Sometimes it's as though we've become chaplain to our friends, colleagues, family. We're the listening ear, the compassionate heart. It may not be appropriate to talk about Jesus every day with people we see so regularly, but we know that people are watching us and that we're communicating Jesus in the way we treat them. Zoë agrees:

> My everyday 'mission/evangelism' may not mean sharing my faith all the time to every person I meet. I prefer a more natural approach, just making friends with people, loving them, being kind, thoughtful. I've found that some of the short-term mission projects I've been involved with in the past haven't shown any sign of longevity; I've not seen lasting fruit. But I've seen that longevity, fruit that lasts, in my friendships. I have built relationships with people, some over months, some years now. I didn't go into them with an 'I wanna convert you' attitude, though! People aren't stupid . . . they see right through your Christian jargon!

How can you make a habit of communicating God's love to your people of peace?

LOVING POWER

When Jesus shared the good news with groups or individuals, the message was often accompanied by miracles. People were healed or set free from demonic oppression, a powerful demonstration of God's love. When He commissioned the disciples in Mark's Gospel, Jesus said that miracles would accompany the believers.[8]

This continues through the Acts of the Apostles. The Holy Spirit is poured out on Pentecost and people hear the gospel in their native language, there are healings, exorcisms, visions and dreams. The message is complemented, not compromised, by the signs and wonders taking place.

It's challenging when we look at Scripture intending to imitate Jesus! Perhaps it's time to be that walking, talking overflow of heaven that Martin described? Now it seems that the healings and miracles more often happen inside the church in meetings, rather than out there in the world. Are we keeping the good stuff to ourselves again?

Stephanie* was one of my neighbours, and I'd meet her in the park from time to time as we pushed our babies around the park. Stephanie had recently remarried and had two children from her first marriage. Blended families often have to negotiate a number of adjustments, but one of Stephanie's daughters found it especially painful – so much so that she was getting ill on a regular basis. She'd seen countless doctors, but all they could say was that it was stress related. The next few times I saw Stephanie, I knew I needed to ask if I could pray for her daughters, but I was way too scared. I'd just found a mum to go walking with; I didn't want her to think I was a nutter. Anyway, eventually I asked Stephanie if I could pray for her family, thinking that she'd give me a few

*Stephanie's name has been changed.

requests. Instead she put her hands together, closed her eyes and bowed her head. As we prayed, something broke. Stephanie had carried huge amounts of guilt concerning the end of her marriage and its effect on her children. It became clear that God wanted to touch Stephanie just as much as her daughter as we prayed.

I didn't see Stephanie for months after that, and I wondered what had happened. Finally, I bumped into her in the grocery store. When I asked how the family was doing, she said that since we prayed together that morning, all the symptoms of her daughter's illness left her. Isn't God good?

There are many people in our communities who would say that while they're not religious, they are spiritual. People are interested in spiritual things; some have had spiritual encounters (positive or negative), dreams or visions that are simply unexplainable. Iyabo and I met at our summer jobs at a high street shoe store and became great friends. She was fascinated by a range of spiritual ideas like numerology, astrology and new age practices. She was also interested in Jesus, but He was no more significant than any other spiritual figure. Once, when she was sick, I'd offered to pray for her healing. When she said she was better, I was so excited and explained to her that Jesus had healed her. Her response? 'Well, I got all my friends from different religions to pray for me, so I figured one of them would work!'

For years it seemed as if nothing changed; Iyabo was always a brilliant friend, but my faith was, as she said, 'great for you, Jo', but not relevant to her life at all. Then, over a six-month period, wherever she went, she heard someone call her by name. It was a clear voice, pronouncing her name with a distinct Yoruba (Nigerian) accent. It was so loud that she'd turn and look to see who was calling her, only to see people having private conversations, or even speaking in another language. She was freaked out! As she became more interested in Jesus, the voice got louder. Finally she heard a testimony from someone who said, 'You don't have to listen to anything I've said to you. Just listen to Jesus.' Iyabo was overwhelmed. She recognised that Jesus was the one who was calling her; who had been calling her to Him all along. It was time to find out why. That afternoon she called me and said, 'Heaven. Hell. God. Jesus. Tell me everything. Now!' She became a Christian on the phone that day.

Stu, a young professional, has found that praying for people and sharing testimonies about God's power at work is having a huge impact on his workplace.

Miracles are an awesome way of sharing the kingdom with workmates as they make people listen and are a demonstration of God's love. I've found that it's love that makes people wake up to God.

Every Monday morning when my team at work asked how my weekend was, I gave them a summary of the miracles I'd seen that weekend. Initially, they'd all go quiet, but as the months passed, people became more interested. Finally people began to ask for prayer, or if I knew someone was sick, I'd offer to pray with them. For some the healing has been total and instant. Others have experienced partial or gradual healing. All of them were amazed at God's healing power, and it has made it so much easier to talk about God!

I'm constantly amazed at how receptive people are to prayer, either to be prayed with, or prayed for. I forget how desperate the human condition can get, especially without Jesus. Without Jesus there is no lasting peace or hope. There is no Saviour. Why wouldn't you want a miracle?

Here are some habits to cultivate:

- The Bible is the perfect place to start. Read Jesus' ministry in the Gospels and Acts of the Apostles, see the amount of

people who came to faith through encounters with God.
- Look and listen out for signs of God speaking to people already. Sometimes people will mention their dreams or spiritual encounters, because they consider you 'spiritual'. Are you prepared?
- Pray for your people of peace, let them know that you pray for them, ask if they have any requests.
- If there is a prayer team at your church, find out how you can get involved. It's a great training ground for ministering to people outside the church.
- If not, see what other resources are out there. I've found John Wimber's *Power Evangelism* particularly inspiring!

BE AVAILABLE

Opportunities to share our faith come in different ways, if we're open to them. There are people of peace at work, but also sitting next to us on the bus. They are at the hair salon, or they might be installing something at our house. There are both the fleeting opportunities and the opportunities within more established relationships, if we're watching and available for God to use us. Could we cultivate a new habit, simply to be more available to share our faith?

- Remember Jesus sent His disciples out in teams. Who's on your team, praying for you, encouraging you, even being physically with you at times as you reach out?
- Ask God, 'Show me one person I can speak to today – give me one clear opportunity and I will take it.'
- Take a week at work. Deliberately make yourself more available to serve anybody in the workplace.
- Take one month and make yourself available for every day

of that month, agreeing with God that you are the light of the world and the salt of the earth, and that you have a message worth sharing! Keep a journal and see how God uses you.

- Have you considered a short-term mission trip?
- Invite your person of peace to church. It could be for a special event, or for an Alpha course, or it could just be that it's Sunday!

LIFESAVERS

When I've seen friends come to faith, I wonder why I don't talk about Jesus more often! Like everyone else, I get distracted and busy. I miss the opportunities, or I feel indifferent or unprepared. Developing a few habits can help keep this part of our spirituality alive, help us keep introducing people to Jesus.

Remember the person who introduced you to Jesus? They introduced you to a Saviour who forgave you and set you free. They set you on the journey of a life with God. They changed your life for ever. Now you have the opportunity to do the same for others: with spirituality that's real and saves lives. You can't get better than that.

Epilogue: Keep running

Therefore, since we are surrounded by such a great cloud of witnesses, let us throw off everything that hinders and the sin that so easily entangles. And let us run with perseverance the race marked out for us, fixing our eyes on Jesus, the pioneer and perfecter of faith. For the joy set before him he endured the cross, scorning its shame, and sat down at the right hand of the throne of God. Consider him who endured such opposition from sinners, so that you will not grow weary and lose heart.
(Hebrews 12:1–3)

I came so they can have real and eternal life, more and better life than they ever dreamed of.
(John 10:10 *The Message*)

Can Jesus transform a person's life? Yes He can; even though our lives are so different, our personalities so diverse. He offers us more than a decision to believe in Him; He longs to transform our hearts. He longs for more than a fan club; He calls us to be His followers. It's an arduous path, a narrow way, the road of transformation. We'll need to practise this journey, train for it, until, by His grace and power, we get there. Still, we're not the first to run this race. Christians throughout history have trodden this path as they've sought to navigate their way through life and culture and all their challenges. Now it's our turn . . .

It's 6.30 a.m. in Central Phoenix. At the point where Central Ave meets Bethany Home Road is Murphy's Bridle Path. It's a popular, well-known road with many fans. Murphy's Bridle Path is a peculiar dirt track which serves as the pavement for a road lined with mature ash and olive trees, beautiful homes and architecture. Yet, if you're a runner or hiker, the beautiful homes and the fancy cars are irrelevant. All you see is the dirt track. You're more than a fan; you're a follower who knows its tread. It's all the beauty you need. And you start running.

You're not the first to run this race. This is one of the city's ancient roads, in honour of one W. J. Murphy, a pioneer who built the Arizona Canal, established the citrus industry and built a path. It once accommodated carriages for people. But today people are too busy, too preoccupied for this path. It holds an historical, traditional fondness, perhaps even cultural nostalgia, but it's not personally meaningful, not now. Unless you're a runner.

I'm not the greatest runner who ever lived, but I want to be on this road. So I start running. Most of the Phoenician population drives everywhere. We runners are something of a minority, a peculiarity, especially on the days when the desert heat is at its most brutal. The goal is clear. Regardless of the circumstances, keep running.

Some people are cheerful runners, smiling as people pass by, greeting everyone they meet. Others seem to be locked into their own world. They may be alongside you, but this is alone time, they don't say 'hello', and you don't take it personally.

There are those who stand out on the road. The elderly stand out. There's a guy with the broadest smile who raises his hand and says a grand 'Good morning!' And a woman who shuffles, almost staggers her way along the road. Her smile is almost . . . grateful. There's something special about them. They've jogged, run and walked along this path for a long time now. And their smiles reveal that they understand that clocking speeds is not the point of this particular path. It's the fact that they're still here, still moving forward after all this time. They laugh like nobody else does, because they aren't just hoping to make it. They *know* where they're going.

Sometimes I see teenagers. Always dressed differently from everyone else, their very style indicates that we live in different worlds. They seem to have this mix of self-consciousness and perhaps a little bit of defiance as they make their way down the road. And when they look you in the eye, they read you. I've always thought they seem the loneliest. But they're on the path.

My race is nothing spectacular; I'm just trying to make it. Some days I'm focused and sharp and I know where I'm going, or think I do. Other days I'm more aware of my vulnerabilities in the desert heat. I have this backpack which is a water bottle. I used to leave it at home because I wanted to look as if I had it all together. Now I know I won't make it without extra resources to refresh and sustain me.

I'm the smiler on the road. I like to make eye contact with other runners, wave a little! But even then some days it's too much, too hard. Once, when I was about to stop, a woman appeared from nowhere and we talked and ran together. Her presence refreshed me as we shared our goals, and helped me log another mile without thinking. Another morning my body was in agony. I thought I might be injured and for some reason I felt so useless. An older woman smiled and said to me, 'I am so proud of you!' I nearly burst into tears because I didn't realise how much I needed to know I was doing OK. I keep running.

All the runners are different: different ages, colours, shapes and sizes. There are some serious runners out there who are lithe, fit, strong and fast. I admire them, and sometimes imitate their pace. It's great for a while, but I can't keep up with them. I'm reminded that they have a different race to run from me. Being inspired by someone else's experiences is one thing, but comparing and evaluating yourself in the light of someone else's race is another. Surely what matters is that we're all on the path, headed in the same direction?

The gritty dirt trail holds a certain appeal, but so do the magnificent houses. Occasionally they present a beautiful distraction. I imagine myself in that home, or driving that car. The kids would love that beautiful garden. I didn't realise I was dissatisfied until now. My mind begins to wander and I forget what I'm there for. Most of the times that I've tripped and fallen over were not because I was tired. It was because I was distracted and had taken my eyes off the path. One fall was particularly spectacular, leaving me bruised, bloodied and aching. It took a while to get up from that one, but I did. I stumbled until I could walk, and I walked until I could jog, then I jogged until I could run again.

I'm not the greatest runner. I have good days, bad days, dull, bored, average days that are nothing to speak of. There are days when all I see is the dirt path beneath me, or times when all I can think of is the pain my body is in, or the sweat that stings my eyes. But there are days when, just a couple of miles along, where Northern Ave and Orangewood meet, I look up and see Piestewa Peak, the mountains. So I keep running.

Besides, I'm not the only one. There's a group of us, a community, who have chosen the dirt trail instead of the easy road to travel on. We've chosen the unglamorous, peculiar, bumpy 'ancient' road to chart our steps. We take it at different paces, in different ways, but we're all there together. We're in it together. And tomorrow we'll all be there again, on the path, doing the same thing.

Keep running.

Notes

Introduction

1. Ronald J. Sider, *The Scandal of the Evangelical Conscience* (Baker Books, 2006).
2. ibid. p. 13.
3. Luke 12:42.
4. Luke 12:48.
5. Luke 12:48 *The Message*.
6. John 10:10 *The Message*.

Chapter 1

1. Psalm 139:13–14 NLT.
2. In 1983, Dr Malcolm Gardner, a Harvard professor, introduced his concept of 'multiple intelligences' in *Frames of Mind: The Theory of Multiple Intelligences* (William Heinemann Ltd, 1984). Gardner argued for a broader view of intelligence and consequently suggested that there are eight different potential learning styles.
3. Proverbs 4:23.
4. Mark 7:20–3.

5. Matthew 9:9.

6. The Greek word for 'follow' used in this verse comes from *akoloutheo*: *a* – 'in union with', *keleuthos* – 'a road'.

7. Ideas from Mike Breen and Steve Cockran, *Building a Discipleship Culture* (3Dimension Ministries, 2009), www.3dministries.com.

Chapter 2

1. John Ortberg, *The Life You've Always Wanted* (Zondervan, 2002), p. 43.

2. Matthew 11:29.

3. 1 Timothy 4:7–8 *The Message*.

4. Dallas Willard, *The Great Omission* (HarperOne, 2006), p. 61.

5. Matthew 11:29.

6. Matthew 28:18–20.

7. Ideas from Mike Breen and Steve Cockran, *Building a Discipleship Culture* (3Dimension Ministries, 2009), www.3dministries.com.

8. Hebrews 12:1–3.

Chapter 3

1. Mark 8:33.

2. Mark 8:34.

3. Mark 8:35.

4. In Luke's account of this story, Jesus calls his listeners to take up their cross daily (see Luke 9:23).

5. See Matthew 16:24.

6. Mark 8:35–7 CEV.

7. Dietrich Bonhoeffer, *The Cost of Discipleship* (SCM Press, 1937), p. 44.

8. Romans 12:1–2.

9. www.methodist.org.uk/index.cfm?fuseaction=opentogod.content&cmid=1499.

Chapter 4

1. Matthew 5:43–4.
2. Mark 11:25–6.
3. Luke 6:36–7.
4. Luke 17:4.
5. Matthew 18:32–3.
6. Matthew 18:35.
7. Romans 5:6–10.
8. Corrie ten Boom, *The Hiding Place* (Hodder & Stoughton, 1972), p. 221.
9. Isaiah 53:4–5.
10. Matthew 6:14–15.
11. Matthew 5:44.
12. Matthew 18:15–17.

Chapter 5

1. Proverbs 13:12.
2. Proverbs 14:10.
3. Psalm 56:3.
4. Psalm 55:4–5.
5. Psalm 42:5.
6. Ruth 1:21.
7. Psalm 22:1.
8. Psalm 13:5.
9. Isaiah 53:3.
10. From 'When Silence Falls', 29th Chapter with Tim Hughes, 2006.
11. From Matthew 1:23.

Chapter 6

1. *Newsweek* magazine, 5 January 2009.
2. Data taken from *Newsweek*, ibid.
3. James 1:17.

4. John 10:10.
5. Revelation 12:11.
6. Philippians 4:4–8 NLT.
7. Philippians 4:4 NLT.
8. Philippians 4:5–6.
9. 1 Thessalonians 1:6; 2:14.
10. 1 Thessalonians 5:16–18.
11. 1 Samuel 7:12–13.
12. Philippians 4:7–8 NLT.
13. See Acts 16:22–34.
14. John 14:26–7.
15. Philippians 4:9.
16. 'Come Thou Fount of Ev'ry Blessing', Robert Robinson, 1758.

Chapter 7

1. Mark 10:21.
2. Thomas Merton, *The Wisdom of the Desert* (Norton, 1970), p. 3.
3. 1 Timothy 4:7.
4. 1 Timothy 4:16.
5. Gordon Mursell (ed.), *The Story of Christian Spirituality* (Fortress Press, 2001), p. 367.
6. Mark 6:31.
7. C. S. Lewis, *The Screwtape Letters* (Fount, new ed. 1998).
8. Luke 5:16.

Chapter 8

1. Ben Campbell Johnson, *Living Before God* (Eerdmans, 2000).
2. Gary Chapman, *Five Love Languages* (Northfield, 1995).
3. Exodus 31:1–6.
4. Brother Lawrence, *The Practice of the Presence of God* (Hodder & Stoughton, 1981), p. 59.
5. Psalm 139:23–4.

6. 2 Timothy 3:16–17 *The Message*.
7. Richard Foster, *Life with God* (Hodder & Stoughton, 2008), p. 62.
8. For a more detailed explanation of *Lectio divina*, see Richard Foster's *Life with God*, or www.contemplativeoutreach.org, and www.couk.org.uk.
9. Gene Edward Veith, *Loving God with All Your Mind* (Crossway, 2003), p. 11.
10. Romans 12:1.
11. Bob Rognlien, *Experiential Worship* (NavPress, 2005).

Chapter 9
1. Seth Godin, *Tribes* (Piatkus, 2008), p. 3.
2. Genesis 1:26.
3. Mark 3:14 (emphasis added).
4. John 13:23.
5. John 13:8 *The Message*.
6. John 13:14–15.
7. Acts 2:42–7 *The Message*.
8. Thanks to Mal for his contribution to these ideas.
9. Luke 9:23.

Chapter 10
1. 1 Samuel 23:16–17.
2. Timothy Joyce, *Celtic Christianity* (Orbis, 1998), p. 45.
3. 1 Corinthians 4:16–17.
4. Esther 4:13–14 NLT.
5. Psalm 71:17–18.
6. For a full list of the Huddle questions, get a free download on www.3dministries.com, in the 'Shop' section.

Chapter 11
1. Revd Dr Martin Luther King, *Stride Toward Freedom*

(Ballantine, 1958), pp. 28–9.

2. Zechariah 7:9–10.
3. Isaiah 58:6–7.
4. Amos 5:23–4.
5. Luke 4:18–19.
6. Matthew 28:19–20.
7. Quoted in Gordon Mursell (ed.), *The Story of Christian Spirituality* (Fortress Press, 2001), p. 318.
8. Matthew 5:13–14.
9. John Stott, *Involvement: Being a Responsible Christian in a Non-Christian Society* (Fleming H. Revell, 1985), p. 101.

Chapter 12

1. John 15:16 (emphasis added).
2. 2 Corinthians 12:9.
3. Luke 10:5–7 NIV.
4. A more detailed exposition and understanding of Jesus' person of peace strategy can be found in Mike Breen and Steve Cockran, *Building a Discipleship Culture* (3Dimension Ministries, 2009), www.3dministries.com.
5. John 10:10 *The Message*.
6. Romans 1:16.
7. 1 Peter 3:15–16.
8. Mark 16:20.